English *for* HUMAN RESOURCES

SHORT COURSE SERIES

Pat Pledger

Cornelsen

Impressum

Verfasser:	Pat Pledger, Hamburg
Berater:	Beth Negus, München Pete Rutherford, Düsseldorf
Projektleitung:	Meike Kolle, Rebecca Syme
Außenredaktion und Koordination:	James Copeland
Redaktionelle Mitarbeit:	Mindy Ehrhart Krull
Layoutkonzept:	finedesign, Berlin
Technische Umsetzung:	zweiband.media, Berlin
Umschlagsgestaltung:	Jan Haux / Pepe Jürgens, Berlin

Quellen
Titelfoto © Fotolia, vege | **S. 3** © Shutterstock, Mathias Rosenthal – © Shutterstock, Andresr – © Shutterstock, Rawpixel – © Shutterstock, Pressmaster – © Shutterstock, Sfio Cracho – © Shutterstock, Tyler Olson | **S. 5** © Shutterstock, Mathias Rosenthal – © Shutterstock, Andresr – © Shutterstock, Rawpixel – © Shutterstock, Pressmaster – © Shutterstock, Sfio Cracho – © Shutterstock, Tyler Olson | **S. 6** © Shutterstock, Mathias Rosenthal | **S. 9** © Shutterstock, dotshock | **S. 11** © Shutterstock, iDraw | **S. 13** © Shutterstock, Pixsooz | **S. 14** © Shutterstock, Andresr | **S. 15** © Shutterstock, Sergey Korkin | **S. 16** © Shutterstock, iDraw | **S. 19** © Shutterstock, adriaticfoto | **S. 20** © Shutterstock, adriaticfoto | **S. 23** © Shutterstock, docstockmedia | **S. 24** © Shutterstock, Rawpixel | **S. 25** © Shutterstock, Pressmaster | **S. 26** © Shutterstock, Micolas | **S. 28** © Shutterstock, Zurijeta | **S. 30** © Shutterstock, iDraw | **S. 32** © Shutterstock, ndoeljindoel | **S. 33** © Shutterstock, jesadaphorn | **S. 34** © Shutterstock, Pressmaster | **S. 35** v.o.: © Shutterstock, michaeljung – © Shutterstock, Stephen Coburn – © Shutterstock, wernerimages – © Shutterstock, Andrey_Popov | **S. 39** © Shutterstock, Pressmaster | **S. 40** © Shutterstock, Monkey Business Images | **S. 43** © Shutterstock, Sudowoodo | **S. 44** © Shutterstock, Sfio Cracho | **S. 45** © Shutterstock, LDprod | **S. 46** © Shutterstock, iDraw | **S. 49** © Shutterstock, bikeriderlondon | **S. 51** © Shutterstock, Monkey Business Images | **S. 52** v.o.: © Shutterstock, Tyler Olson – © Shutterstock, Steve Cukrov | **S. 54** © Shutterstock, i4lcocl2 | **S. 55** © Shutterstock, iDraw | **S. 56** © Shutterstock, Pressmaster | **S. 58** © Shutterstock, Dusit | **S. 59** © Shutterstock, El Nariz

www.cornelsen.de

1. Auflage, 1. Druck 2015

Basierend auf English for Human Resources ISBN 978-3-464-20481-8

Alle Drucke dieser Auflage sind inhaltlich unverändert und können im Unterricht nebeneinander verwendet werden.

Druck: AZ Druck und Datentechnik GmbH, Kempten

ISBN: 978-3-464-20342-2

PEFC
PEFC/04-31-2260

PEFC zertifiziert
Dieses Produkt stammt aus nachhaltig bewirtschafteten Wäldern und kontrollierten Quellen.

www.pefc.de

Table of Contents

Introducing *English for Human Resources*

English is an essential part of working in human resources today. This is especially true as companies expand and form more international partnerships, with English as the common language of global business. For those working in an HR department or as an independent HR specialist, this book will help build stronger relationships with colleagues and business partners.

English for Human Resources has been specifically designed to help you build confidence when using English as part of your professional life. The book's six units cover the topics, skills, and vocabulary that will help you develop your competence in situations such as recruiting, hiring, describing benefits, managing contracts, conducting performance reviews, mediating conflicts, enabling professional development, and handling labor negotiations.

- The units are built on realistic scenarios that draw from a range of situations and highlight different ways of communicating, such as meetings, phone calls, emails, and informal conversations. A variety of exercises accompany these excerpts to allow you to put the skills and phrases you have learned into practice.
- Listening exercises in each unit, found on the accompanying CD, are a key feature of the book and provide you with vital listening practice. They feature a range of accents to help your listening skills and reflect the way English is spoken as a lingua franca in business.
- The book encourages you to practice your human resources skills with other people in your English course or with your instructor. The Partner Files exercises give you the opportunity to immerse yourself in realistic situations while practicing key skills and language.
- In the back of the book you will find a comprehensive list of useful phrases to refer to when doing the communicative exercises as well as in your professional life. Transcripts for the listening activities, an Answer Key, an A–Z Wordlist, and Model Correspondence are provided to assist you as you work through the book.

The Needs Analysis on the next page will support you when using the book. It will help you set personal learning goals and assess your progress as you work through each unit.

I hope you enjoy using the book and that it helps you develop your skills and build your confidence.

Pat Pledger

Needs Analysis

English for Human Resources is designed to improve your ability to use English in your professional life. However, you are in the best position to know what language and skills you need to develop to help you in your work.

Look at the lists below and spend a few minutes selecting the items that you consider most important. Which do you want to prioritize and improve? Add other items that you would like to concentrate on to the lists.

Human Resources language and skills

	have made good progress	need more practice
Recruitment and selection		
☐ Writing job descriptions	☐	☐
☐ Setting up a meeting	☐	☐
☐ Interviewing candidates	☐	☐
☐	☐	☐
☐	☐	☐
☐	☐	☐
☐	☐	☐
Employee relations, development, and assessment		
☐ Discussing the terms of a contract	☐	☐
☐ Writing an offer letter	☐	☐
☐ Handling staff problems	☐	☐
☐ Giving performance reviews	☐	☐
☐	☐	☐
☐	☐	☐
☐	☐	☐
Compensation, benefits, and labor relations		
☐ Explaining benefits packages	☐	☐
☐ Reviewing salaries	☐	☐
☐ Negotiating with unions	☐	☐
☐	☐	☐
☐	☐	☐
☐	☐	☐

Try to keep the language and skills you want to improve in mind while working with the book. Once you have completed the book, turn back to this page and assess your progress.

In this unit you will …
- review job descriptions and person specifications
- practice exchanging information and making suggestions
- read about methods of recruitment

1 Recruitment

Put the recruitment tasks in the order you think they normally occur. Compare your results with a partner.

- ☐ a Create or update the job description.
- ☐ b Make a job offer.
- ☐ c Prepare a person specification.
- ☐ d Advertise the job online.
- ☐ e Shortlist applicants from the first interviews.
- ☐ f Conduct second interviews.
- ☐ g Carry out assessments and interviews.
- ☐ h Select the most suitable candidate.
- 1 i After an employee resigns, analyze the job and consider alternatives for hiring a replacement (e.g., assigning responsibilities to existing staff).
- ☐ j Send feedback to unsuccessful applicants.

In the above example, an employee resigns. What other reasons are there to look for new staff?

1 **Job descriptions and person specifications are two important HR documents. What types of information do they include? Put the items into the correct column.**

~~competencies~~ | main purpose of job | desirable skills | key duties / responsibilities | skills and qualities needed for job | practical requirements (shift work, travel, etc.) | qualifications/training | ~~job title~~ | previous experience | location | reporting relationships (who person is responsible to and for)

Job Description	Person Specification
job title	*competencies*

Job Description and Person Specification

The purpose of a **job description** is to outline the scope and responsibilities of a specific job. An effective job description outlines the job's main duties and how it fits into the company's hierarchy and operations. A **person specification** describes the ideal candidate for a specific job. The person specification lists skills, experience, competencies, and other information. One purpose of both documents is to give candidates a realistic sense of how well they match the position.

2 **Label the sections of the job description with headings from the box.**

Essential experience · Job overview · Job title · Key duties / responsibilities · Location · Reports to · Responsible for

JOB DESCRIPTION

.... 1 Training Manager – UK

.... 2 General Manager, UK and Northern Europe

.... 3
- A small team of UK trainers
- 2 administrators
- 1 administrative assistant

.... 4
- To design, develop, and oversee general training programs for UK-based team, with particular emphasis on IT- and sales-related training.
- To work closely with branch managers on developing team-building and monitoring effectiveness.

.... 5
- To design and put into effect new training courses and record results to identify future needs of the company.
- To prepare a staff training manual for use at all branch offices.
- To carry out an initial training audit and prepare a report on findings with ongoing suggestions for improvement.
- To be responsible for the annual UK training budget, to report to the board annually, and to work within the agreed budget.
- To visit all branch offices regularly in order to train branch managers, review ongoing training, and assess customer service.
- To report weekly to the General Manager, UK and Northern Europe.

.... 6
- Training management and evaluation experience.
- Management and coordination of team of trainers.
- Budget management.

.... 7
- Based in Manchester.
- Requires traveling within Great Britain and Northern Ireland (e.g., to visit branch offices and carry out training programs).

Words you need

to assess beurteilen
audit Prüfung
board (of directors) Vorstand
branch Filiale
to carry out durchführen
manual Handbuch
to monitor kontrollieren
to oversee beaufsichtigen, leiten

3 Read the following statements about the job description on page 7 and mark if they are true or false. Correct the false statements.

	True	False
1 The job is based in Northern Ireland and doesn't require much traveling.		
2 The training manager is responsible for three people.		
3 The job is for someone with an extensive training background.		
4 The training manager reports directly to the board of directors.		
5 The training manager is responsible for conducting an audit of training requirements and preparing a new training manual.		

Best Practice

The language of job descriptions

Keep job descriptions simple so that they are easy for job applicants to understand. Avoid complicated phrases, company jargon, and abbreviations. Here are some useful verbs to use when explaining key responsibilities:

to **develop** general training programs
to **work** closely with branch managers
to **put into effect** new training courses
to **prepare** a staff training manual
to **assess** customer service
to **foster** creativity

Other verbs often used in job descriptions include:

to conduct	*durchführen*
to contribute	*beitragen*
to deliver	*liefern*
to ensure	*gewährleisten*
to establish	*aufbauen*
to implement	*umsetzen, einführen*
to involve	*umfassen*
to liaise	*in Kontakt sein*
to maintain	*aufrechterhalten*
to manage	*leiten*
to monitor	*kontrollieren*
to provide	*zur Verfügung stellen*
to support	*unterstützen*

Remember:

- people work **for** or **at** a company
- they work **in** a department or team
- they are responsible **for** other staff and **for** (doing) their work
- they are responsible **to** or accountable **to** their boss/manager/supervisor

4 Choose the correct verbs to complete the sentences.

1 The training manager **reports to | manages | monitors** the general manager.
2 A suitable applicant must be able to **develop | work | implement** closely with branch offices and **establish | construct | support** a good rapport with managers.
3 We will **develop | manage | evaluate** the professional development needs of our staff, and then, based on those results, we will **contribute | develop | train** new training courses.
4 There is a certain amount of hands-on work which involves **conducting | ensuring | contributing** training courses for the UK-based team.
5 First you need to **maintain | prepare | operate** a new staff training manual.
6 UK branch offices need to be supported, so the job **maintains | ensures | involves** a lot of traveling.

The phrase "good rapport" (pronounced "rah-por") is a common way to describe a positive relationship based on good communication.

5 **Match 1–6 with a–f to form phrases that describe the competencies of a manager.**

1	build	a	staff performance
2	foster	b	an effective team
3	ensure	c	staff
4	identify	d	creativity
5	improve	e	problems
6	motivate	f	deadlines are met

To "be competent" or "have competence" refers to the ability to do something, e.g., "Susan is highly competent at giving presentations."

A "competency" is a special ability, attitude, or behavior critical to success in a job, e.g., "Multi-tasking and good people skills are key competencies for this position."

6 **Decide where the section headings go in the person specification.**

Additional information · Skills and qualities needed for job · Desirable skills · Competencies · Previous experience · Qualifications/training

PERSON SPECIFICATION
Training Manager – UK

............1
- Educated to degree level or equivalent experience
- Language skills in French and German preferable

............2
- At least five years' experience in a management-level training role at an IT or high-tech company
- Member of recognized training organization(s)

............3
- Team-building and ability to motivate staff
- Creative and resourceful in designing materials and manuals
- Preparation and implementation of training budgets and audits
- Monitor staff performance throughout the organization
- Maintain open lines of communication on all training issues with managers and board

............4
- IT experience and knowledge of relevant software
- Customer care and quality control experience

............5
- Strong communication skills
- Ability to interact effectively at all levels of the organization
- Active decision-maker and self-starter
- Intercultural awareness

............6
- Must be willing to travel frequently
- This is a progressive role with opportunities for promotion in the US and Europe

Words you need

preferable vorzuziehen
promotion Beförderung
resourceful einfallsreich

7 Match the phrases from the person specification with the definitions.

decision-maker · intercultural awareness · open lines of communication · quality control · self-starter · team-building

1 .... someone with initiative, motivation, and resourcefulness
2 .... creating unity and enthusiasm within a group
3 .... a sensitivity for different backgrounds and lifestyles
4 .... a system for testing and maintaining standards
5 .... someone who evaluates options quickly and chooses with confidence
6 .... ongoing and clear sharing of information

8 02 **Listen to the conversation between Lisa Woodlow, head of HR at the UK office of a large European manufacturing company, and Robert Brown, a recruitment associate. Tick the types of recruitment sources they mention.**

- ☐ national/local newspapers
- ☐ company website
- ☐ online job portals
- ☐ executive search / recruitment agency
- ☐ job fairs
- ☐ networking / social media
- ☐ in-house recruitment
- ☐ trade journals

9 02 **Mark whether the following statements about the conversation are true or false. Listen again to check.**

		True	False
1	Lisa is handling the recruitment of staff in Berlin.	☐	☐
2	Thomas Scholz is the general manager of the Berlin office.	☐	☐
3	The HR manager they are looking for must have two-to-five years' generalist HR experience.	☐	☐
4	Applicants should have either a qualification in human resources management or a university degree.	☐	☐
5	English is not important for the job.	☐	☐
6	Robert is confident that they will have good applicants from inside the company.	☐	☐
7	The German magazine for HR professionals doesn't publish job advertisements.	☐	☐
8	Robert is offering interviews in the UK and in Berlin.	☐	☐
9	They are looking for an HR manager because of a recent merger.	☐	☐
10	Lisa will conduct the interviews.	☐	☐

10 **Put the words into the right order to make phrases from the dialogue.**

1 have | moment | do | a | you
2 English | must | highly | they | in | be | proficient
3 agree | sure | there | with | I'm | you | not | I
4 step | you | I'm | ahead | of | one
5 things | you | under | clearly | control | have

11 **Match the words and phrases from the conversation (1–8) with their meanings (a–h).**

1 keep s.o. posted
2 disciplinary procedures
3 have a word (with s.o. about sth.)
4 merger
5 trade journal
6 sign off on sth.
7 internal
8 generalist

a discuss
b give official approval for sth.
c opposite of a specialist
d inside a company
e when two companies become one
f publication for a specific profession
g keep s.o. informed
h policies for handling employees who are breaking the rules

Now use the words and phrases 1–8 to complete the sentences from the conversation. Use the correct forms.

Lisa I just wanted to .... A with you about the search for an HR manager in Berlin. How's that going?

Robert Well, the job description and person specification have both been finalized, and Thomas Scholz in Berlin .... B them. We're looking for someone with two-to-five years' .... C HR experience.

Robert Well, firstly on the company intranet, on the European careers page, although I don't think there's much chance of finding a(n) .... D candidate.

Lisa I'm not sure I agree with you there. Don't forget we took on a lot of employees with the .... E in 2014.

Lisa OK, sounds good. By the way, I believe there's a German .... F for HR professionals.

Lisa Yes, good idea. Well, Robert, you clearly have things under control. .... G as you move forward.

Robert No problem, will do.

Lisa All right, thanks. I've got to run now, actually. I have a meeting about .... H in about five minutes.

12 **Complete the following sentences with words related to the root words *employ* and *recruit*. You might need to add prefixes or suffixes and change the form.**

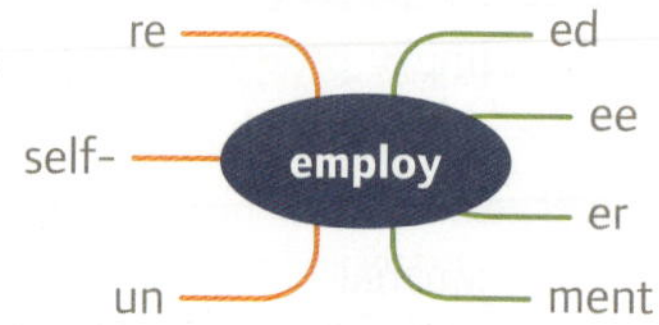

employ	1 We are unable to hire people who are *self-employed* unless they work for several different companies. 2 There are more people on the job market when levels of ………………………… are high. 3 She told her ………………………… she was looking for another job. 4 We hired six new ………………………… in the last quarter. 5 We ………………………… her in the same position when she returned from maternity leave.
recruit	6 Last year we ………………………… two team leaders for our call center. 7 We've revised our overall ………………………… procedure because of new labor laws. 8 We are currently ………………………… four new IT consultants.

13 **Match the different sources of recruitment (1–8) with their definitions (a–h). Which sources does your company use to find new employees? Which sources do you think are most effective?**

1 networking
2 internal announcements
3 company career pages
4 job sites
5 social media
6 print ads
7 headhunters / recruitment agencies
8 unsolicited applications

a professionals specializing in matching jobs with candidates
b online portal for job listings
c job listings in newspapers and trade magazines
d inquiries made by an individual to a company
e vacancies posted on the company website
f online networking sites
g announcing vacancies to other employees in the same company
h sharing information through personal interaction

14 **Work with a partner to practice making suggestions. Use phrases from the box.**

▷ Partner File 1: Partner A, page 60 / Partner B, page 63

Phrases to use

Exchanging information
- Can we have a word about …?
- I'd like to be up to date on what's happening.
- So where/what are you planning to …?
- What are your thoughts on …?

Making suggestions
- I suggest we …
- In my opinion …
- What do you think about …?
- Well, we should consider …

Agreeing and disagreeing
- I agree. / I disagree.
- I think so too.
- Thanks, that's a great point.
- Yes, good idea.
- I'm not sure I agree with you there.

Recruiting in the 21st Century: Five Major Developments

Shifts in technology, society, finance, and demographics have all changed the way that HR departments manage their recruiting. Here are five major developments that are revolutionizing how recruitment is done today.

1. Social Media

There are more than one billion people on social media today. Almost every candidate for a corporate position has a social media presence or an Internet footprint of some kind. HR departments that disregard this information simply cannot be competitive in today's environment.

2. The Science of Assessment

Human assessment is a science that is constantly changing. The Myers-Briggs Type Indicator is one tool that has been around for decades, but now there are hundreds of other personality or skills assessments. An explosion of new companies that are developing assessment software is changing pre-hire assessment in a radical way. Candidates are completing computer tests that are faster and more accurately gauging their abilities.

3. Applicant Tracking Systems

Known as ATS for short, an applicant tracking system is the basic database used by HR offices for gathering, organizing, and analyzing information about job applicants. In fact, it's such a basic tool, you might think it could never be changed. Think again! This is an aspect of recruitment that recruiters frequently find tedious and repetitive. By streamlining systems, the ATS in today's HR departments is much easier for everyone to use, and has much more robust analysis abilities.

4. The New Candidate Experience

Remember: technology is a two-way street. When you make systems easier to use for recruiters, they should be made easier for candidates, too. Today's job applicant expects a clean, efficient, stress-free experience when interacting with a company. If that experience is not provided, it's a guarantee that some of the best candidates will be turned off – and may even end up working for one of your competitors!

5. The New Role of Recruitment Agencies

For a while, everyone thought that headhunters would go the way of the dodo bird. With the rapid expansion of the Internet, who needs a middleman? But it's precisely this vast amount of available data that makes the recruitment agency more essential than ever: headhunters are the professionals that know how to sort through and interpret all of the information available, analyze it most efficiently, and help you find just the right person.

Words you need

to disregard vernachlässigen
to streamline rationalisieren
tedious lästig, ermüdend
vast riesengroß

Over to you

- Have you observed other recent developments in how recruitment is done? Besides technology, what factors have influenced these changes?
- The article emphasizes the value of a positive candidate experience. Do you agree that this is an important aspect of effective recruiting? Why or why not?
- Does your HR department often try out new recruitment methods? In your opinion, is frequent experimentation useful for HR departments?

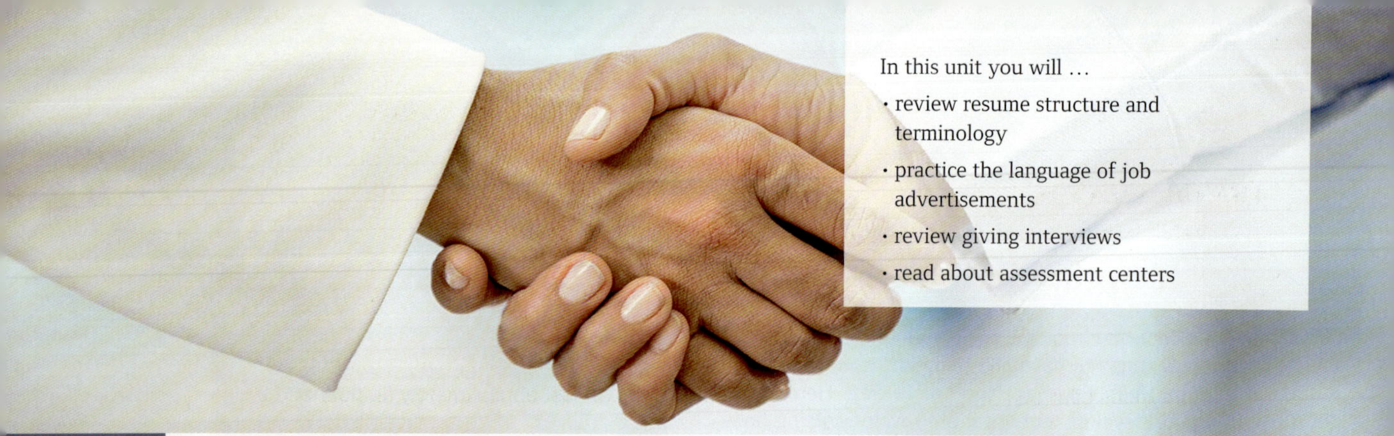

In this unit you will …

- review resume structure and terminology
- practice the language of job advertisements
- review giving interviews
- read about assessment centers

2 Selection

Work with a partner. Decide whether you agree or disagree with these statements about job applications and interviews.

		Agree	Disagree
1	A resume should be no longer than two pages.		
2	It's good practice to include a photograph with a resume.		
3	It isn't necessary for applicants to put their date of birth on their resume.		
4	Written references that candidates supply with their applications could be false, so they shouldn't always be trusted.		
5	Applicants should enclose official copies of degrees, certificates, and exam results with a job application.		
6	Applicants should include salary expectations as part of a job application.		
7	Applicants should never wear jeans to an interview.		
8	At an interview, it is appropriate to ask female applicants about their plans for starting a family.		

The word "Lebenslauf" can be translated as "resume" (American English) or as "curriculum vitae" or "CV" (British English).

Note that "resume" is pronounced "rez-oo-may".

1 Read the job advertisement on the following page, and then match the verbs from the ad (1–8) to the correct definition (a–h).

1 to create a good rapport
2 to understand the customer's needs
3 to provide advice
4 to promote a range of services
5 to attend an interview
6 to be notified of the outcome
7 to receive a shift allowance
8 to be entitled to a benefits package

a to receive additional incentives on top of salary
b to get extra money for working certain hours, e.g., at night, on the weekend, or during holidays
c to suggest the best way to do something
d to discuss a job opportunity with a manager or HR representative at a company
e to develop a positive relationship through good communication
f to be told the results of a decision
g to attract customers to what your company offers
h to recognize what the customer wants

TRAVEL CONSULTANTS
JETWINGS HEAD OFFICE, BRIGHTON

The Image
At JetWings, we're renowned for our high standard of customer service, and we know that first impressions count.

Our Travel Consultants are responsible for creating a good rapport with our callers, understanding their needs, and providing advice and assistance for all their travel needs. Consultants have a wide variety of responsibilities and play a key role in promoting JetWing's ever-expanding range of services, while always maintaining a high level of customer service.

The Demands
Speaking to around 100 callers each day, you need to be a self-starter while maintaining high levels of accuracy in this fast-paced and dynamic environment. Your shift pattern will have a variety of start and finish times, including some early mornings and late nights. Don't forget, shift work means you might have to work weekends and holidays.

The Interview
The interview process consists of a group interview at an assessment center. The interview will last approximately an hour and a half, after which you'll take part in a series of practical exercises. Our recruitment assessors will monitor your performance and look for specific competencies, such as managing customer demands, teamwork, and attention to detail. If you're successful in the group stage, you'll be asked to attend an individual interview with two recruitment assessors. The results of this final stage will be sent to you by email.

The Rewards
The starting salary is competitive and, as a shift worker, you'll also receive a shift allowance. There's also an increase to the base salary after successful completion of a six-month trial period. As a JetWings employee, you'll be entitled to a generous benefits package, including a holiday allowance, pension plan, life insurance, and JetWings concessionary travel.

2 Some applicants had questions about the job. Write out answers to the questions.

1 "What are the main responsibilities of the job?"

2 "What are the hours of work?"

3 "What types of competencies might help me get the job?"

4 "As a shift worker, do I receive extra payment?"

5 "What should I expect during the interview process?"

6 "Does anything change after the trial period is over?"

Words you need

base salary Grundgehalt
concessionary ermäßigt
fast-paced schnelllebig
trial period Probezeit
range Sortiment, Angebot
renowned renommiert
shift allowance Schichtzuschlag

3 **Put the main headings into the order in which they might appear on a resume.**

a Education
b Skills and Achievements
c Personal Profile
d Training and Development
e Professional Experience
f Personal Details

4 **What details would you expect to find on a resume? Complete the boxes with items from the box. Add one item to each category.**

academic qualifications • brief summary of work history and abilities • dates of previous employment • exceptional performance ratings • full contact details • internships • key achievements in previous positions • language skills • ~~name~~ • nationality • previous employers • ~~publications~~ • qualifications or certificates from on-the-job training • relevant training courses attended • responsibilities in previous positions • seminars attended • soft skills

Education	Skills and Achievements	Personal Profile
	publications	

Training and Development	Professional Experience	Personal Details
		name

5 Read the email and label it with the following items (a–j).

a invitation to an interview
b acknowledgement of the applicant's email
c polite ending
d subject of the email
e signature
f contact details for arranging an interview
g salutation
h complimentary close
i procedure if invited to a second interview
j additional person to receive the email

From: Heather Murphy
To: Caroline Dugard
Cc: Liz Winston ___ 1
Date: August 25
Subject: Application for Call Center Team Leader ___ 2

Dear Ms. Dugard, ___ 3

Thank you for your resume and email of August 9th applying for a team leader position in our call center in New York. ___ 4

We currently have two vacancies for team leaders and we would like to invite you for an initial interview at our New York office in the next two weeks. If successful, you will then be asked to attend a full-day assessment center with seven other applicants next month, after which a final decision will be made. ___ 5

We will pay your travel expenses to the interview and to the assessment center if selected. During the assessment center, which will last from 9:00 a.m. to 5:00 p.m., lunch with the other applicants and assessors will be provided. If you need overnight accommodation, we will book a hotel near our office. Full details of the assessment center procedure will be sent to you in advance if you are selected. ___ 6

Please call Liz Winston at 212 845 9554 ext. 2317 to arrange a convenient time for the interview. Please find attached an application form which we would like you to complete and bring along to the interview. ___ 7

We wish you luck at the interview and look forward to welcoming you to our New York office. ___ 8

Yours sincerely, ___ 9
Heather Murphy
Recruitment Manager
NewMobile Ltd.
newmobile-ltd.com ___ 10

6 Tick whether the statements are true or false. Correct the false statements.

		True	False
1	Caroline has applied for a position as call center assistant.		
2	She sent a resume with her email.		
3	The whole recruitment process will be completed within two weeks.		
4	The company will pay for Caroline's journey to the interview.		
5	Applicants will be told what the assessment center procedure involves when they get to the company.		
6	They want Caroline to complete an application form and send it back to them.		

7 **Put the sentences from an email into the correct order. Then check your answer with the model email on page 77.**

a ☐ We would like to invite you to attend an interview at this office. I would be grateful if you could call me at 0044 0675 23144 as soon as possible to arrange a suitable time.
b ☐ We look forward to meeting you.
c ☐ Thank you for your email of September 2, applying for the position of …
d ☐ If you have any questions, please raise them when you call to arrange the interview.
e ☐ Alternatively, you can go to our website for these documents and other information about the company. A map showing the location of our office is also attached.
f ☐ Attached is a copy of the person specification and job description, which we would like you to familiarize yourself with before the interview.

Did you know?

General rules for business correspondence	Salutation	Complimentary close
When you don't know the person's name	Dear Sir or Madam:	Sincerely,
When you know the person's name	Dear Ms./Mrs./Mr. Brownley,	Yours sincerely,
When you know the person well	Dear James,	Best regards, / Best wishes, / Yours,

8 03 **Listen to the telephone conversation and fill in the gaps to complete sentences from the dialogue.**

1 I was asked to phone you to .... a time.
2 So, can you .... to see us for an .... interview next week?
3 .... that won't be possible.
4 I could come the week after that, ...
5 Can you .... on Wednesday the 10th at 4:00 p.m.?
6 Yes, ... 4:30 p.m., then.
7 You can .... at home and bring it along with you to the interview.
8 We .... to meeting you.

Phrases to use

Setting up a meeting

What date would be convenient for you?
What time would suit you / works for you?
Would Monday at 10:30 suit you / work?
Is March 5th at 6:00 p.m. convenient?
How about 10:00 a.m.?

Tuesday the 8th of July would be good for me.
Monday's bad for me, I'm afraid.
That sounds great.
Yes, that would be good for me.
I think that should be possible.

9 Work with a partner to practice setting up a meeting. Use phrases from the box on page 18.

> Partner File 2: Partner A, page 60 / Partner B, page 63

Did you know?

When a company employs new staff, they are *hired* (AE) or *taken on* (BE). When these employees then decide to leave, they *resign* or *hand in their notice/resignation*; more informally, they *quit*.

When employees have to leave because they did something wrong, they are *dismissed* or their contracts are *terminated*; more informally, they are *fired* (AE) or *sacked* (BE). If they have to leave because a company can no longer employ them (e.g., due to bankruptcy or downsizing), the employee is *let go* (AE) or *made redundant* (BE) or even *offered early retirement*.

When an employee is *laid off (to lay off)*, it is sometimes only temporary (for a season or because of a drop in production), but it often becomes permanent.

A "pensioner" is someone who receives a "pension", while a "retiree" is someone who has "retired" or is in "retirement". Someone who has stopped working because of illness or handicap is "on disability".

10 **Complete the sentences with expressions from the box.**

1 My best marketing assistant just .... Unfortunately, we couldn't match the offer she received from the other company.

2 Will we be able to .... a replacement when John hands in his .... ?

3 The project can't continue in these freezing temperatures, so we'll have to .... six workers until the end of February.

4 As for those staff who can't relocate to the new factory in the north, will they be .... ?

5 I heard one of our retail associates has been .... for stealing, is that right?

6 Head office has just issued a new policy that all employees over 63 will be ....

11 04 **You'll hear extracts from Caroline Dugard's interview with recruitment manager Heather Murphy. Listen to the first extract and match the numbers to what they represent.**

five	days a week
eight	years in previous company
seven	team leaders
ten	years with present company
six	call center associates

05 **Listen to the second extract and tick the call center problems they discuss.**

1 Difficulties with customer complaints
2 Staff shortages
3 High absenteeism
4 Staff relationships
5 Stress

06 **Now listen to the third extract and tick the sentences you hear, either in Column A or Column B.**

	A	B
1	I particularly enjoy dealing with customers.	I enjoy dealing with particular customers.
2	I have the ability to write a good report with people on the telephone	I have the ability to build a good rapport with people on the telephone.
3	It's a thing that comes naturally to me.	It's something that comes naturally to me.
4	My partner has a good job in this area.	My partner has no job in this area.
5	My company hasn't asked me if I would like to relocate.	My company has asked me if I would like to relocate.

12 **What do the words and expressions used in the interview mean? Tick the correct definition.**

1 to fill someone in
- a to complete a form
- b to give someone more information so he/she has all the details

2 to be promoted
- a to move to a higher position in the company
- b to take a lower position in the company

3 to outline something
- a to summarize
- b to give a detailed explanation

4 to complain
- a to say everything is fine
- b to say that you are unhappy about something

5 policy
- a a rule
- b a special person who deals with something

6 to relocate
- a to move to a new area (with your job)
- b to be asked to leave your job

13 Use the form to make notes about the interview. Listen again or refer to the transcripts on pages 66–67 if necessary. Do you think Caroline should be shortlisted for the assessment center? Complete gap 10 with your own ideas.

Interview Notes

Name: (1) *Caroline Dugard*

Job applied for: (2) ....

Date of interview: September 10th

Experience

a 5 years' experience in a similar position.

b (3) ....

c (4) ....

Level of responsibility

a reports directly to call center supervisor

b (5) ....

c (6) ....

Specific abilities

Staff relationships (7) ....

....

Customer service: good communication skills, (8) ....

....

Reason for leaving

(9) ....

....

Suitability for the position

Caroline appears to have the right qualifications and experience to carry out this position. Her communication skills and relationship with staff (10) ....

....

....

Recommendation for shortlist to assessment center: Yes __ No __

Forming interview questions

The interviewer in Exercise 11 uses open questions, which cannot be answered with *yes* or *no*. Below are some examples of how to word your interview questions to get people talking about themselves and their experience.

What …?
What aspect of your job do you like best?
What do you know about …?
What experience have you had with …?

How …?
How do you go about dealing with …?
How would you handle …?

Why …?
Why do you want to leave your present job?
Why did you deal with the situation in that way?

OR
I'd like you to tell me …
Could you give me an example of …?
Interesting. What else do you …?
Could you tell me a little more about …?

14 Change these closed questions (which can be answered with *yes* or *no*) to open questions.

1 Do you have a good rapport with your present supervisor?
2 Have you handled many staff problems in your current job?
3 Do you consider yourself good at customer service?
4 Are you used to working shifts?
5 Are you able to work on your own initiative?
6 Do you work well under pressure?

Now match a–g with 1–7 to form the open questions you heard in the interview between Heather and Caroline.

1 So, could you tell me about your
2 What exactly
3 Could you outline some of the problems
4 Could you expand on that
5 And how do you deal with
6 What aspect of your job do you
7 Why do you want to leave

a a little more?
b like best, Caroline?
c does that involve?
d experience as a team leader in your present job?
e you've dealt with as a team leader?
f your present job?
g difficult customers, or with customers who have a complaint?

15 **Make a list of questions you would ask at an interview for your own job. Then exchange your list with a partner and practice asking and answering the questions in an interview situation. Try to use the phrases in the box for establishing rapport and asking follow-up questions.**

Phrases to use

Establishing rapport

Thanks for taking the time to come in today.
Perhaps we can start with you walking me through your resume.
Please feel free to ask any questions you may have.
I'm going to start by … and then we'll talk about …
Finally, we can deal with any points you would like to raise.

Asking follow-up questions

Could you tell me some more about …?
What exactly do you mean by …?
Could you expand on that?

16 **Complete the sentences with words related to the root words. You might need to add prefixes or suffixes and change the form.**

apply	1 There were two *applicants* .... who were far better than the others in terms of previous experience. 2 All candidates must complete an .... form to bring to the interview. 3 The employment legislation is not .... to people working less than 25 hours per week.
select	4 As we had a lot of candidates for the advertised position, we were able to be very .... 5 We offer a .... of benefits to our staff in addition to the base salary.
assess	6 In some types of recruitment, ... centers are used regularly. 7 It was difficult to .... the final two shortlisted applicants, as they had such different skill sets.

What to Expect at an Assessment Center

Assessment centers use a variety of ways to test candidates. Here are some of the most common exercises.

- **Information Sessions.** These are short, introductory presentations designed to give candidates more information about the organization and available positions. The information provided may be needed in interviews and exercises later, so candidates are encouraged to ask questions and take notes.

- **Interviews.** Even candidates who have been interviewed before may face additional one-on-one or group interviews at the assessment center. Recruiters are likely to use the opportunity to hold more in-depth discussions with candidates, who might even find themselves speaking with potential colleagues and supervisors.

- **Personality Inventories.** These are written tests used to evaluate the candidate's personality and how he/she reacts to complex situations. Unlike other assessments, a personality inventory isn't timed or graded. In fact, it has no right or wrong answers, but is used to determine how well the candidate will fit within the corporate culture, and what he/she envisions as an ideal working environment.

- **Psychometric and Aptitude Tests.** These are classic intellectual aptitude tests. Candidates are given a limited period of time to complete a series of multiple-choice questions that are designed to test a wide variety of logic problems. In some cases, the test may be tailor-made for the relevant job opportunity and will cover both basic and specialized skills.

- **Inbox Exercises.** The candidates sit down in front of a computer that shows an email inbox. In a limited period of time, they have to work through the emails by taking notes, writing responses, and fulfilling requests. These exercises test skills such as prioritizing, writing ability, delegating, and referring questions to supervisors when necessary.

- **Case Studies.** In these exercises, a small team of candidates are given a file folder containing documents relating to a particular situation. They are asked to review the documents and work together to make a presentation in which they recommend a detailed course of action. The subject matter itself isn't important, as the candidates are being tested on their ability to work as a team, process large amounts of information, exercise judgment, and make clear and rational decisions in a high-pressure situation.

Words you need

aptitude Befähigung
folder Mappe
in-depth detailliert
tailor-made maßgeschneidert

Over to you

- What other assessment center exercises do you know of? Which ones do you think are most effective?
- Which exercises do you think are best administered by computer? Do you think it's possible to design an assessment center where candidates complete all exercises on a computer?
- What types of jobs are best suited for testing candidates in assessment centers? Are there any jobs for which assessment centers should not be used in the recruitment process?

In this unit you will …

- review common phrases used in employee relations
- practice the language of contracts
- review writing offer and rejection letters
- read about mediation in the workplace

3 Employee Relations

Here are some common collocations (word partnerships) that apply to employee relations. Some of the letters are missing. Complete the words, and then match the collocations with the definitions on the right.

1 s_ _ dis _ _ _ m _ _ _ t _ _ n
2 em _ _ _ _ m _ _ t con _ _ _ ct
3 _ qu _ _ pay
4 par _ n _ _ l l _ _ ve
5 workp _ _ _ _ inj _ _ _ es
6 s _ ort-t _ m _ w _ rk _ _ g
7 disc _ pl _ n _ _ y and gr _ _ van _ e procedure
8 w _ _ k-re _ _ ted st _ ess

a reduced working hours, usually when a company has a decrease in production
b accidents that happen at work
c to treat a person unfairly because of one's gender
d the time parents can take off when they have a baby or adopt a child
e the same salary for men and women
f stress caused by negative factors in the job
g steps to follow when an employee breaks the rules or wishes to challenge a decision
h written details given to an employee to confirm terms and conditions of a job

1 **Match the blue words with red words to form basic terms and conditions that appear in job offers. The blue words always come first.**

Example: annual salary

expense ~~annual~~ vacation benefits relocation trial/probationary period leave ~~salary~~ package sick paid

Are there other terms and conditions that appear in job offers in your country? Discuss with a partner.

Did you know?

The practice whereby employees can choose exactly what time they start and finish work is called *flexible working*, *flexible hours*, or *flextime* (AE) / *flexitime* (BE).

2 07 **Laura Braun has just been offered a position at a British company. A recruitment manager, Nancy Dodds, and a team leader, Gabe Hartman, are discussing the job's terms and conditions with her. Listen to the conversation and decide whether the statements are true or false.**

		True	False
1	Laura will be working flexitime in her new job.		
2	Overtime is paid and cannot be taken as time off.		
3	She will be paid only for the first 12 weeks if she is ill.		
4	Her holiday entitlement is 20 days per year for the first two years.		
5	She sent in details for her references with her application.		
6	She hasn't told her employer in Hamburg she's leaving yet.		

The words "vacation" and "holiday" have the same meaning, and the terms "paid vacation" (AE) and "holiday entitlement" (BE) are identical.

Likewise, "ill" and "sick" have the same meaning and are used interchangeably.

3 **Match 1–6 with a–f to form sentences from the dialogue.**

1 I'm afraid we don't
2 We'd like to tell you
3 I'm sure that won't be an issue,
4 By the way, we're currently looking
5 Let's start with
6 If you're ill, we expect you

a as it's only a week.
b about the conditions of employment.
c to let us know as early as possible.
d your hours.
e at more flexible working arrangements.
f offer flexitime yet.

4 07 **Listen to the dialogue again and fill in the missing words. The first letter and a clue at the end are given.**

1 There may be *o*............ during busy periods. *(longer hours than normal)*

2 This is either paid or given as *t*............ *o*............ in lieu. *(when you are not working)*

3 Your *a*............ paid holiday is 20 days. *(per year)*

4 We'll be *c*............ your previous and current employers. *(to get in touch with)*

5 The offer of employment is *s*............ to satisfactory references. *(conditional on)*

5 **Complete the puzzle with words from the dialogue.**

ACROSS

3 The .... letter is the official letter sent to a successful applicant
6 Official written agreement
7 The standard .... is 40 hours. (two words)
8 A printed document with company information and policies

DOWN

1 Letter from previous employer verifying good employment record
2 Days off are called "paid ...."
4 "My .... employer in Hamburg knows I'm leaving."
5 Many companies have a standard application ....

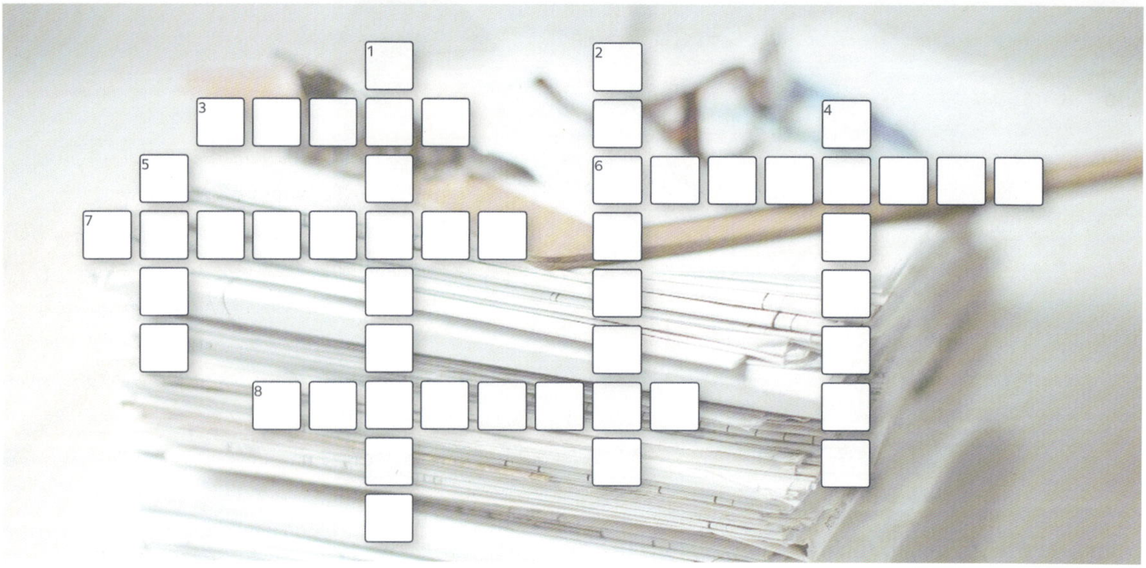

6 **Complete the table with words and phrases from the box.**

~~annual leave~~ · dismissal · flextime (AE) / flexitime (BE) · full-time employment · paid vacation (AE) / holiday entitlement (BE) · part-time employment · public holiday (AE) / bank holiday (BE) · redundancy · relocation expense · resignation · ~~shift work~~ · sick leave · six-day week · ~~trial period~~

Work patterns	Terms of contract	Time away from work	Ending employment
shift work	*trial period*	*annual leave*	

Compare your table with a partner and try to add words to each category.

7 Complete the sentences with words related to the root word *flex*. You might need to add prefixes or suffixes and change the form.

flex

1 Our company has a very .... policy for employees who need time off for childcare.

2 We've offered .... in the company since the early 2000s.

3 There is little or no .... for our staff in terms of hours of work, as they have to be in the office during regular business hours.

4 Unfortunately, our managing director is quite .... about deadlines.

8 Look at the list of points that should be mentioned in an employment contract. Match each point (1–10) to the extracts from model contracts (a–j).

1 start date
2 rate of pay, when and how paid
3 normal hours of work, overtime, shift patterns
4 days off
5 job title (or a brief description of the job)
6 workplace location
7 notice period
8 sick leave
9 pension plan
10 disciplinary rules and grievance procedure

a The amount of notice you are required to give or be given by your employer is four weeks.

b A copy of the company's disciplinary procedure is attached to this contract and employees are asked to read it carefully.

c Your annual salary will be €45,000, payable monthly in arrears by credit transfer to your bank.

d Your normal place of work will be the above address. From time to time the company may require you to work at other sites on a temporary basis.

e Your employment begins on 5 January.

f The company does not offer a pension plan but provides access to an investment fund. Details can be obtained from the HR department.

g Major public holidays are observed. If you are required to work on a public holiday, you will be entitled to time off in lieu.

h You must inform the office by 10:00 a.m. on the first day of absence due to illness. Failure to do so may lead to disciplinary action.

i Normal hours of work are 37.5 per week, 9:00 a.m. to 5:30 p.m., Monday to Friday, with one unpaid hour for lunch each day.

j Your current job title and responsibilities are detailed in Appendix I and may be amended from time to time. You will be notified of any changes in writing.

Words you need

to amend (ab)ändern
to be entitled to sth. Anspruch auf etw. haben
disciplinary action Disziplinarverfahren
grievance Beschwerde
in arrears rückwirkend

Did you know?

Companies contribute to their employees' pension plans in different ways.

Two common options are *defined benefit* and *defined contribution* schemes. A defined benefit scheme is a commitment by the company to pay an employee a certain pension following retirement, based on a formula that accounts for age, salary, years of service, etc. In a defined contribution scheme, the employee builds up a fund based on ongoing paycheck deductions and employer contributions.

In the US, many employees have a *401k account*, which is a savings plan that allows employees to save a portion of their salary without paying taxes on it. Many employers will match the employee contribution.

Phrases to use

The language used in contracts of employment is highly formal and includes fixed phrases, formal vocabulary, and the use of passive and the *will*-future.

Fixed phrases
payable monthly in arrears
failure to do so
subject to disciplinary action

Use of formal vocabulary
to amend = to change
to be entitled to = to have the right to
to notify = to tell

Use of passive
employees are asked …
you may be required …
details can be obtained …
more information can be found in …
employees are expected …

Use of future
your place of work will be …
any changes will be discussed …

9 **Complete the sentences with words and phrases from the box.**

are asked · are entitled to · are expected · ~~can be found~~ · may be required · notified in writing · payable monthly in arrears · subject to disciplinary action

1 Full details regarding sick leave *can be found* .... in the staff handbook.
2 You .... to work in another office of the company from time to time.
3 Employees .... to work overtime as and when required.
4 You'll be .... of any changes to your contract.
5 You .... four weeks' holiday per annum after completion of six months' probation.
6 Your salary is .... on the last day of each month.
7 Employees .... to notify the company of any absence due to illness by 10:00 a.m. on the first day.
8 You may be .... if you fail to do this.

10 **Decide if the paragraphs (a–j) are from an offer letter or a rejection letter, and then put them into the correct order.**

Offer letter	Rejection letter
d	g

a We would like you to start on 1 February, if possible. During your first week, you will participate in an introductory seminar to familiarize you fully with the company. Full details of this will be sent to you nearer to the date.

b Thank you for attending the interview for the above position. It was very nice meeting you.

c We're pleased to offer you the position of International Marketing Assistant in the UK Marketing Department, based at the above address, at a commencing salary of £42,000 per annum. This offer is subject to our receiving satisfactory references from your present and past employers and to the satisfactory completion of a three-month probationary period.

d Dear Ms. Grau,

e We appreciate your interest and would like to take this opportunity of wishing you every success in your future career.

f Please let us know as soon as possible if you would like to accept by signing and returning one copy of the enclosed contract. We will then take up your references. We very much hope to have you as a member of the team, and we look forward to hearing from you.

g Dear Mr. Chevalier,

h We have now fully considered your application and regret we are unable to offer you a second interview on this occasion.

i Normal working hours are 9:00 a.m. to 6:00 p.m., Monday to Friday, including an hour for lunch. It will be necessary for you to work overtime as and when required. Holiday entitlement is 20 days per annum, rising to 25 after two years' service. Normally, holidays cannot be taken during the probationary period. All terms, conditions, and benefits are detailed in the enclosed handbook and contract.

j We will keep your application on file and let you know if a suitable opening occurs in the future.

Now look at the words and phrases from the letters above, and match the highlighted words (1–8) with their synonyms (a–h).

1 a commencing salary of …
2 the offer is subject to our receiving …
3 probationary period
4 accompanying details
5 per annum
6 are detailed in …
7 to familiarize
8 we will keep your application on file

a enclosed
b become knowledgeable about
c starting
d year
e conditional on
f laid out
g in our records/database
h trial

11 **Work with a partner to practice discussing terms and conditions of employment. Use phrases from the box.**

> Partner File 3: Partner A, page 61 / Partner B, page 64

Phrases to use

Giving information
I'd like to tell you something about …
Please ask about anything you are not sure of.
I'm sure that won't be a problem.
I'm afraid we don't …

Requesting information
Could you tell me …?
Would it be possible to …?
Could you please let us know …?
Would you mind telling me …?

12 08 **Listen to a presentation by an HR consulting firm, and then complete the sentences.**

1 Even in the best-run companies, there are many .... problems that can ....

2 When someone starts in a new position, he or she is entitled to a written .... laying out the main .... of their employment.

3 All employees have the right to be .... by another employee or a union ...., if applicable, to any disciplinary hearing.

4 Employees must be fully informed of their inappropriate .... and given an .... to explain themselves.

Words you need

to accompany begleiten
disability Behinderung
harassment Belästigung
hearing Anhörung
to take into account berücksichtigen

The word "mobbing" is not used in English. Instead, English speakers use the words "harassment" or "bullying". Other words are "victimization" and "intimidation".

Now discuss the presentation and the following questions.

1 What procedure do employees in your company follow if they have a grievance? What role, if any, does the works council *(Betriebsrat)* play?
2 What are some of the problems that can lead to disciplinary action?
3 What disciplinary procedure is in place where you work?

13 **Read the headlines from articles on HR issues. In pairs, decide what you think they refer to, and then discuss your answers with the whole group.**

1 **Managing Recurring Sickness Absence**

2 **Leadership Positions for Women – Ceiling is Believing**

3 **Dads in Need of Office Role Models**

4 **Diversity Not a Black and White Issue**

5 **Disappearing Ink: Tattoos Increasingly Banned in Workplace**

6 **Wellness Management – A Growing Necessity?**

7 **Miss Manners Needed for Millennials in the Workplace**

8 **Open-Plan Offices Popular Again (Except with Employees)**

Which of these subjects have arisen in your company? How did you deal with them?

14 Rank the workplace stress factors (1 = not stressful, 5 = extremely stressful). Compare your results with a partner.

		1	2	3	4	5
1	interpersonal relationships at work (dealing with coworkers)					
2	tight deadlines (pressure to get work done in a short amount of time)					
3	pressure from supervisors					
4	work environment/equipment (quality of working conditions)					
5	workload					
6	job security (fear of losing one's job)					
7	working hours					
8	low autonomy (excessive supervision)					
9	repetitive work					
10	work/life balance					

What health and safety measures is your company taking to reduce stress levels in staff?

15 Which of the health and safety measures are typical of factories, offices, or both? Work with a partner to add items to the list.

		Factories	Offices
1	carry out fire drills		
2	prevent exposure to harmful substances		
3	provide eye exams		
4	post safety signs		
5	provide safety equipment (hard hats, etc.)		
6	do risk assessments		
7	train employees in first aid		
8	wear protective clothing		

Which measures have been introduced in your workplace?

DOs and DON'Ts for Successful Mediation

Conflict happens. It happens in all areas of business. And if these issues aren't dealt with, there can be serious consequences. Morale drops. Good people quit. Profitable relationships dissolve. Great companies go under. Clearly, too much is at risk to allow conflict to go unresolved in the workplace.

The HR manager can help by identifying conflict and intervening at the right moment with a formal mediation process. Surveys have shown that once a conflict gets to the disciplinary and grievance stage, it generally becomes more difficult to resolve.

Here are some tips on what to do – and what not to do – in workplace mediation:

DO ...

... keep it specific. For example, ask each participant to describe three or four things they'd like to see resolved. One employee might say, "I'd like Laura to submit her figures by Friday morning so I can complete my weekly report on time. That would reduce a lot of stress for me."

... keep it clean. All participants should treat each other with dignity and respect. It's okay to have reasonable disagreements over specific issues; it's never okay for a conflict to become overly personal or offensive.

... keep it fair. Let everyone know that you won't take sides. It's not your job to offer a judgment one way or another. Explain that you expect them to work together to resolve the conflict. If they're unwilling to do so, you may be forced to take disciplinary action.

DON'T ...

... avoid the conflict. Hoping problems go away has never been an effective way to solve them. Even if the conflict appears to have been put aside, it will return whenever stress increases or a new disagreement occurs. Indeed, unresolved conflicts tend to resurface at the worst possible moments. If you find yourself thinking, "This will pass with time" – think again.

... meet separately. If you allow each individual to tell their story to you in separate meetings, you risk polarizing their positions. Meet together, and let each party summarize their point of view, without comment or interruption by the other party.

... minimize the conflict. The conflict is real, and playing it down won't help. Why? Because stress spreads, and everyone in your office could be affected. A single disagreement between two people can create a hostile work environment for others. In worst-case scenarios, employees may take sides, and the division will deepen throughout the whole company.

Words you need

to deal with sth. sich um etw. kümmern
dignity Würde
to play sth. down etw. herunterspielen
to take sides Partei ergreifen

Over to you

- What has been your experience with organized mediation in the workplace? Has it been an effective process?
- What other methods can an HR department use to resolve conflicts before they reach the disciplinary stage?

In this unit you will …
- practice handling staff problems
- review the language of performance reviews
- read about cultural diversity

4 Performance and Development

Do you agree or disagree with the statements? Discuss with a partner.

1 "Train people well enough so that they can leave, treat them well enough so they don't want to." –Richard Branson, Virgin Group

2 "I hire people smarter than me and then I get out of their way." –Lee Iacocca, Ford Motor Company

3 "Passion is energy. Feel the power that comes from focusing on what excites you." –Oprah Winfrey, broadcaster

4 "Be a yardstick of quality. Some people aren't used to an environment where excellence is expected." –Steve Jobs, Apple

5 "You cannot push anyone up the ladder unless he is willing to climb." –Andrew Carnegie, U.S. Steel

6 "Leadership is performance. You have to be conscious of your behavior, because everyone else is." –Carly Fiorina, Hewlett Packard

1 **Match the HR practices in the box with their definitions (1–8).**

equal opportunity policies • ~~flexible work arrangements~~ • individual development • mentoring • onboarding process (AE) / induction programme (BE) • performance review • secondment • team development

1 *flexible work arrangements* .... adapting working hours and location to suit the diverse needs of employees' lives
2 .... temporary transfer to another organization or part of the company
3 .... continually advancing the professional development of employees
4 .... regular evaluation of an employee's performance, development requirements, and potential
5 .... maintaining fair working practices for each employee
6 .... motivating a group of employees to work together effectively
7 .... providing an employee with an experienced person who can assist with professional development and offer support and advice
8 .... informing new staff about the company and its procedures to help them to settle successfully into their new jobs

Which of the practices does your company use? Which do you think are most effective?

2 Read what four people have to say about staff problems, and complete the gaps with words from the box.

colleagues · complained · courses · participates · regulations · situation · supervisor · trouble

A Helen, shop floor team leader

You know, I only started here four months ago but I'm already thinking about leaving. Gerry, the shop floor ....[1], is always correcting me, always telling me that things are done differently here, and he's so negative. He never gives me any real help. And my team doesn't follow my instructions. I just don't know how much longer I can cope. I don't feel in control of the ....[2].

B Carlos, marketing director

Listen, I'm having ....[3] with a major project. I've put together a team of marketing staff from all our different locations, not just here but all over the world, to work together to update our global marketing procedures. The problem is that nobody ....[4] in the meetings and progress is slow. Several members have already asked to leave the project.

C Betsy, department manager

I need help with a problem employee. He's making a lot of mistakes and is argumentative with ....[5]. What's more, he's taken 20 days' sick leave in the last year and other employees are complaining about it. Several clients have also recently ....[6] about his attitude.

D Karl, project manager

I've been here seven years and I desperately need some training on the latest ....[7] and accounting procedures in my field. I'm now coordinating an international project and it's embarrassing that I know almost nothing about EU law. My boss tells me we're too busy for training ....[8], but it's essential that I'm totally up-to-date. What do you recommend? Can you talk to my boss?

In English, we speak of "training courses", "seminars", or just "training". Remember that "training" is always singular (not "~~trainings~~").

🔊 9–12 Now listen to four solutions (1–4) suggested by management. After listening to each solution, decide which problem it applies to from the above texts (A–D).

Words you need

argumentative streitsüchtig
to cope with sth. mit etw. klarkommen
to empower stärken
to enable ermöglichen
field (of work) Arbeitsbereich
to muddle through sich durchwursteln
overdue überfällig

Phrases to use

Making recommendations

- We need to introduce …
- My proposal is to put / is that we put …
- Maybe we should also look into …
- I propose introducing / that we introduce …
- It's essential to take up / that we take up references …
- We still need to …
- I (can) recommend talking / that we talk …
- It's high time (that) we introduced …

3 **Study the phrases for making recommendations above, and then match 1–5 with a–e to form sentences.**

1 I recommend hiring this trainer for
2 True, it's high time that we introduced flexible working arrangements,
3 No matter how much progress has been made, we still need to
4 Having studied the project outline and discussed it with my staff,
5 My proposal is that we promote the workshops

a but it's essential that client needs are still given first priority.
b I recommend that we postpone the project until next year.
c the upcoming seminar on carrying out performance reviews.
d in the next staff newsletter.
e work on providing equal opportunities throughout the organization.

4 **Now use the language at the top of the page to make recommendations. Discuss with a partner what you would recommend for these staff problems.**

1 A female accountant has complained that her salary is lower than two other male employees who do the same work. She was promoted to the job five years ago, is very well qualified, and has been with the company longer than one of the two men.

2 A long-established company has lost some good employees recently because they found it impossible to balance their working lives with the demands of their family life. There is currently no flextime, very few part-time jobs, and only one male employee has taken paternity leave to look after his child due to the negative feeling about such practices.

3 A PR agency that was recommended by existing clients to some multinational companies failed to get two contracts it expected to secure. The reason cited was that their English was not good enough to achieve the desired results. Several staff had asked for English training in the past, but it had been refused.

4 The executive assistant to the CEO went to the doctor complaining of severe pain in his hands and arms. The doctor signed him off work for several weeks. The pain appears to have been caused by prolonged use of the computer.

5 Below are some reasons why companies carry out performance reviews. Write in each heading next to the corresponding reason (1–4).

Engaging staff • Enhancing performance • Opening communication channels • Succession planning

1.	2.	3.	4.
To give positive feedback on what employees are achieving already, enabling them to do their jobs better.	To enable companies to identify potential for future promotion and focus on certain individuals.	To promote better contact between managers and their staff.	To encourage involvement and a sense of personal commitment.

The verb "to succeed" usually means "to achieve", but it can also mean "to follow". The term "succession planning" refers to finding the next person to take over a position. That person is called the "successor", and the person leaving the position is the "predecessor".

6 13 Anna Vollen, a line manager at S.B.C. International, is carrying out an annual performance review with Jordan Howles, an employee from the Edinburgh branch who is on secondment in Vienna for two years. Listen to their conversation, and tick whether the statements are true or false. Correct the false statements.

		True	False
1	Marco was out of the office working on another project.		
2	Jordan was on target despite staffing difficulties.		
3	Anna was in Turkey for two months.		
4	Lara Hoff was unable to put in extra time.		
5	Jordan suggests adding a team member while Marco is away.		
6	Marco has trouble with the level of formality in the office.		
7	Anna thinks the whole team could use cultural training.		
8	Jordan's wife has found a job but isn't happy with it.		

Now put the problems and solutions they discuss next to the appropriate performance goal.

behind because of staff difficulties • check in with each other more often • delegate better • get output up to scratch • have leadership training • meet weekly for a while • raise issues at team meetings • time management • 25% down for six months

Management Skills

-
-
-

Improving Performance

-
-
-

Encouraging Better Communication

-
-
-

7 13 Listen to the conversation again and, using the words in the box, complete the performance review form on Jordan Howles. Decide on the last two action points yourself and then compare them with a partner.

communication · cultural · decrease · delegate · to detail · leadership · long-term sickness · production director · overtime · relationships · skills · training manager

SBC

Performance Review

Name: Jordan Howles
Line Manager: Anna Vollen
Date: 12 December

Job title: Team Leader (bottling)
Location: Vienna
Date of last review: n/a

Strengths:
Attention ....[1], excellent. Accuracy, good.

Jordan feels he doesn't have any problems with staff ....[2].
Wife now in employment of her choice.

Areas to develop:
Jordan doesn't always ....[3] to team members and this causes overwork for himself and thus a ....[4] in output.

Communication ....[5] need attention.

Challenges:
Decrease in output caused by Marco's ....[6], inability of other team members to work ....[7], shortage of staff in the team. Jordan needs to improve his ....[8] with me. Marco needs ....[9] training (as does all the team!).

Action:
1 Speak to ....[10] about:
- temporary transfer of member of staff to Jordan's team.
- ....[11] skills and time management training for Jordan.

2 Talk to ....[12] about cultural training for all of Jordan's team.

3 ....[13]

4 ....[14]

Signed: Line Manager .... Employee ....

8 **Match the expressions from the dialogue with their definitions.**

1 to pay attention to detail
2 to get a little behind
3 to be on target
4 to raise an issue
5 to get something up to scratch
6 to settle in

a to make something as good as expected
b to notice and deal with small individual facts
c to feel happy in a new environment
d to be at the exact level predicted
e to mention something for people to discuss
f to be slower than expected

The language of performance reviews

The purpose of a review is to address past issues and then look forward. Questions posed by the appraiser should always be formulated carefully to avoid upsetting the appraisee during the interview. Being diplomatic and using language to soften disagreement also helps to create a positive environment.

Being diplomatic

- Use *would*, *could* and *may* to make statements less direct: *That would/could/may be very difficult.* (Not: ~~*That's very difficult.*~~)
- Avoid negative words like *terrible*, *awful*, and *very bad*. Instead, use *not very* plus a positive word: *That's not a very positive attitude.* (Not: ~~*That's a terrible attitude.*~~)

Performance review questions

Could you tell me (how things are going with …)?
How do you see (your team developing in …)?
Would you like to give me more details about …?
When did you realize that …?
Would you mind giving me more information on …?
Is there anything else we should talk about?

Softening disagreement

With (all due) respect, I think …
To be quite frank, I don't think …
In all honesty, we should deal with that differently …
I respect your opinion, but …
I'm afraid we can't / I'm sorry, but we can't …
You have a point there, but …
To a certain extent I agree, but …

9 **Improve the statements and questions from a performance review.**

Example: 1 *How do you see the relationship with your team?*

10 **Now work with a partner to practice a performance review with a member of staff who is unhappy in his or her job. Either use the Partner Files or think of a situation of your own.**

> Partner File 4: Partner A, page 61 / Partner B, page 64

Phrases to use

Asking about the job

- I'd like you to tell me how you see your progress over the last year.
- Has there been anything you've found difficult to cope with?
- How are things with the rest of the department?
- What do you like most about your work?

Talking about problems

- Unfortunately, there have been some issues.
- There seems to be a personality conflict between me and someone in the department.
- Well, actually, a member of the department is making life rather unpleasant for me.
- I didn't feel able to talk to you about it earlier.

11 Match the headings to the short descriptions of four training courses.

Time Management

Team Leading from a Distance

Leadership and Team Building

Staff Retention Success

1 ....

Being a competent leader means being able to inspire team members while always meeting your targets. This course covers decision-making, diplomacy, and strategies for working in a diverse workplace.
(eight-hour course over four weeks)

2 ....

Learn tips for setting priorities, managing your workload, and delivering before deadline. Identify what's important and achieve targets and objectives more effectively in less time.
(four-hour seminar)

3 ....

The best employee is the employee that stays through thick and thin. Learn strategies for reducing turnover by boosting morale, responding to the needs of your staff, and creating a dynamic work environment.
(two-day course for managers and supervisors)

4 ....

Running a virtual meeting demands special skills. Learn how to motivate colleagues even when thousands of miles away. Special training for video meetings, conference calls, group emails, and how to optimize use of online document sharing.
(three-hour seminar)

Which course would you send Jordan Howles on? Why? Discuss with a partner.

A reliable employee who stays "through thick and thin" ("in good times and in bad times") can also be described as "dependable", "loyal", or "faithful".

12 Fill in the gaps to form collocations from the course descriptions above.

boosting · colleagues · competent · inspire · managing · priorities · targets · turnover

1 .... leader
2 .... team members
3 meeting your ....
4 setting ....
5 .... your workload
6 reducing ....
7 .... morale
8 motivate ....

13 With a partner, design a one-day time management course for a department in your company. Write an introduction as in the examples above and a short list of the contents. Try to use a few of the word partnerships in Exercise 12.

14 **Complete the sentences with words related to the root words. You might need to add prefixes or suffixes and change the form.**

equal	1 All employees are subject to the same rules, so everybody is dealt with *equally*. 2 The Race Relations Act is about doing away with .... and discrimination. 3 .... pay for men and women is still a big issue in some sectors of business.
diverse	4 We still haven't achieved our goals for increasing .... in the office. 5 The CEO has made it a priority for this year to create a more .... workplace.

15 **Use the phrases in the box to complete the excerpt from a newspaper article.**

in its place • internal change • laying the groundwork • once-a-year • ongoing basis • put an end to

Evimax, a major American insurance company, is making a(n) ....[1] next year that its employees and managers will certainly welcome: it's going to ....[2] the annual performance review.

Adam Wentworth, CEO of Evimax, says the company, which employs tens of thousands of workers in cities around the US, has been quietly ....[3] for this "HR revolution".

The firm will discontinue its five-point ranking system, and will begin to phase out its ....[4] evaluation program during the next fiscal year. ....[5] will be a more fluid system with employees receiving feedback from their managers on a(n) ....[6].

Now answer questions about your experience with performance reviews.

a Describe the review process in your company or a company you know well.
b Describe your last performance review experience.
c Why have some companies decided to stop doing performance reviews?
d Are you in favor of: A) keeping performance reviews in your company the way they are, B) making some changes, or C) ending performance reviews completely?

Compare your answers with a partner. Do you agree about the value of annual performance reviews? What changes do you both think should be made?

Cultural Diversity for Business Success

by Margaret Lewis

Globalization is not just a word we read in the newspaper – it's something we experience in the workplace as well. The typical 21st century office is more diverse than at any period in the past. In response, HR professionals are using new methods to help embrace diversity, manage conflicts when they occur, and channel the benefits of diversity in productive ways.

As a leader in the field of diversity management, I recommend five main strategies for successfully integrating diversity into your business.

1 *Run a cultural status update.* What are the current demographics of your workforce? How many ethnic groups and countries are represented? Share the results with your employees and update the information on a regular basis. Remember that managing diversity is an ongoing project, not a one-time exercise.

2 *Write a statement of intent.* This should be written in positive and clear language, and it should address what your company's leadership wants to achieve in terms of diversity. Make sure that it's endorsed by the top executives and posted in a public place. There's nothing wrong with having a gap between where you are and where you want to be, as long as you're moving in the right direction.

3 *Create a mentorship program.* Employees at all levels in the company may need assistance understanding and working with people from different cultures. Give them an experienced guide to make this possible, and make sure the mentor is actively engaged. Remember, this kind of program requires training and ongoing checks to make sure it's effective.

4 *Hold the top executives accountable.* As with all levels of employees, company leadership can be motivated through regular reviews. Design a performance metric, and evaluate how well the executives create diversity.

5 *Focus on talent and forget about quotas.* The great thing about talent is that it comes from all countries and ethnicities in the world. If you focus on talent in your recruiting, and make a point of looking as widely as possible to find it, you won't have any difficulty building a diverse – and successful! – workforce.

Words you need

to hold s.o. accountable jmd zur Verantwortung ziehen
to endorse befürworten
statement of intent Absichtserklärung

Over to you

- What are the means your company uses to build diversity and to facilitate cooperation between people of different backgrounds?
- Has your company achieved its diversity goals? If not, what key areas does your company need to work on?
- It's sometimes said that "diversity is its own reward". What do you think this statement means? Do you agree or disagree?

In this unit you will …
- practice describing benefits packages
- review the language of salary reviews
- practice using figures and numbers
- read about flexible benefits

5 Compensation and Benefits

Employee benefits are sometimes called *fringe benefits* or *perks*. Working with a partner, add as many fringe benefits to the diagram as you can.

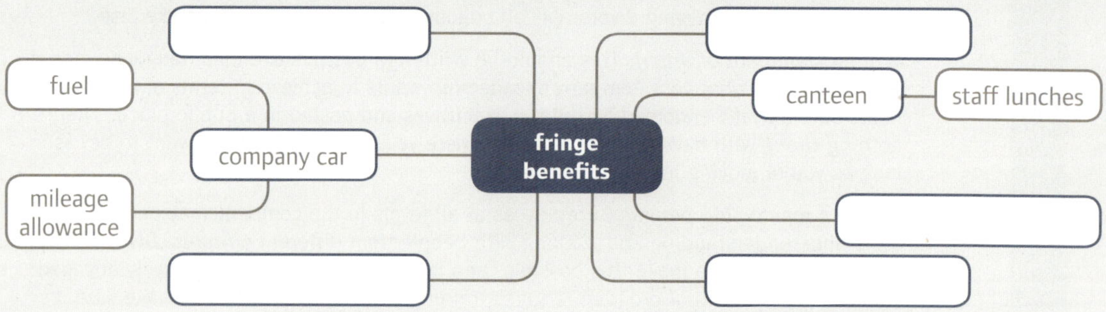

Do you think staff are more motivated by receiving a higher basic salary with fewer benefits or a lower basic salary with a lot of benefits? Discuss with your partner.

1 Use the words in the box to complete the sentences about flexible benefits plans.

choosing/benefits • competitive/package • dual-career/duplicated • pay/tax • sense/control • suit/lifestyle

1 Staff choose the benefits that .... their ...., and as a result they value the benefits more.

2 Staff .... less .... on benefits.

3 A .... benefits .... will help attract and retain key staff.

4 .... couples avoid having benefits ....

5 People can earn more by .... their own ....

6 Employees are given a .... of .... and involvement by being able to choose what is best for them.

Which of the reasons for introducing flexible benefits packages do you consider valid and why?

2 14 **Listen to the departmental meeting between Julie, an HR manager in a multinational company, and her staff, Natalia and Alex. Match the person with the benefit they mention.**

1 Julie			a family-friendly benefits
2 Natalia			b childcare
3 Alex			c profit-sharing bonus

Did you know?

Another term for *pay* or *salary* is *remuneration* or *compensation*. The *salary and benefits* (AE) or *remuneration package* (BE) is the total of all financial and non-financial benefits an employee receives (e.g., salary plus a car, a retirement plan, and life insurance).

3 14 **Match phrases from the three columns to form true statements about the meeting. Listen again if necessary.**

1 Julie called the meeting	a done research	A the new profit-sharing bonus at their next meeting.
2 Natalia felt they needed	b to discuss	B on flextime initiatives.
3 Natalia suggested	c to prepare	C more flexibility for staff.
4 Alex was keen to	d giving	D a summary of benefits and costs.
5 Alex will prepare a proposal	e to inform Natalia and Alex about	E employees more family-friendly benefits.
6 Julie asked Natalia	f to submit	F their benefits package.
7 Natalia has already	g encourage	G staff back to work.
8 Julie is going	h to introduce	H at the next regular meeting.

4 **Add one or two words to complete the phrases from the meeting. If necessary, check the transcript on page 69.**

Phrases to use

Asking for somebody's opinion or ideas

- What's your view on this?
- Could I have your .... [1], Alex?

Clarifying

- What exactly do you .... [2] by …?
- As .... [3], we need …
- I'll .... [4] you in on …

Giving an opinion or feedback

- Yes, I think we need …
- Well, I'm definitely .... [5] of …
- Good idea.
- However, I think we should also .... [6] closely at …

5 Two companies have posted their remuneration packages on the careers page of their company websites. Match the items (a–l) with the benefit descriptions (1–12).

a performance-based pay
b sports club membership
c employee assistance program
d flexible working hours
e relocation expenses
f pension fund
g profit-sharing bonuses
h life insurance
i cafeteria (AE) / canteen (BE)
j childcare services
k shares in success
l salary

Benefits and rewards

We want to attract, motivate, and retain staff by offering the following benefits:

- ☐ 1 A first-class, non-contributory pension plan (i.e., fully paid by the employer).
- ☐ 2 Coverage for your loved ones of four times your annual salary.
- ☐ 3 Free shares after one year's service, dependent on company profits.
- ☐ 4 In-house fitness, sports facilities, massage, and yoga classes, plus 20% off membership to a wide selection of fitness clubs.
- ☐ 5 Daycare.
- ☐ 6 Counseling and advice on personal and domestic issues.

Remuneration package

In return for your contribution to our organization, you can expect a position that offers a collaborative work environment, exciting projects, and a chance to pursue your ambitions within the company, both nationwide and internationally.

- ☐ 7 Depending on job level and experience, we offer competitive compensation to recruit and retain the best staff.
- ☐ 8 Payment is reviewed on a merit basis.
- ☐ 9 You can adjust your working hours to suit personal and family commitments.
- ☐ 10 Paid out twice a year dependent upon business results.
- ☐ 11 Hot meals, salads, and snacks at heavily subsidized prices.
- ☐ 12 Comprehensive moving expenses if you take up a new position or are transferred.

Which package do you personally find more attractive? Why? In your opinion, which package would help retain the best employees at your company?

6 **Use the clues to complete the puzzle and find the hidden word.**

1 .... prices, for example for food, are lower due to company contributions
2 an informal restaurant where you take the food to the table yourself
3 money received regularly after retirement
4 a small part of a company which is bought or given as an investment
5 if you are ...., you stay at the company but move to a different city
6 according to how well you do your job: on a .... basis
7 a synonym for *keep*
8 groups for learning skills or sports

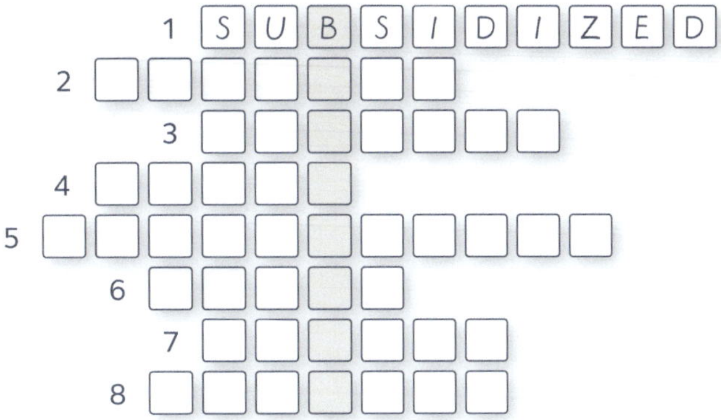

7 **Complete the sentences with words related to the root words.**

benefit	1 We all .... greatly from job satisfaction. 2 People receive sickness and unemployment .... from the government. 3 Your husband is the .... of your life insurance policy in the event of your death.
review	4 Salaries are normally .... annually. 5 We carry out performance .... in September of each year.

8 **Now use phrases from page 45 and from the box below to practice a meeting with your partner(s) about changes to the company's benefits package. Either refer to the Partner Files or think of your own situation.**

> Partner File 5: Partner A, page 62 / Partner B, page 65 / Partner C, page 65

Phrases to use

Agreeing and disagreeing

- I entirely agree.
- I agree with you to a point.
- Yes, but have you considered …?
- I'm afraid I can't go along with that.
- Sorry, but I really can't agree.

Interrupting

- Could I just say that …?
- I'd like to add a point here.
- Excuse me, can I just come in here?
- Sorry, but may I just clarify a point before we go on?

9 **You are writing a short follow-up email to the board of directors about your recommendations. Choose the correct words in each sentence, then put the sentences in the right order.**

Dear Members of the Board of Directors,

a Best/Best wishes[1],
Remuneration Committee

b We appreciate that it will be necessary to hold a detailed meeting about this, but we look forward to hearing your initial/prompt[2] comments.

c We would like to recommend/recommending[3] that the attached proposal be introduced over the next two years.

d If you require any further information/informations[4], please let us know.

e At a meeting of/from[5] the Remuneration Committee last week, the question of a new benefits package has been/was[6] raised.

f We feel this proposal would offer/involve[7] the staff more flexible working arrangements, while benefiting the company in terms of a happy and engaged workforce/workers[8].

"Information" is a non-count noun, which means it never appears in the plural. Other common examples of non-count nouns are "advice", "progress", and "equipment".

10 15 **Listen to Julie talking to a marketing manager, Liam, about salary increases, and connect 1–6 with a–f to form phrases from the dialogue.**

1 we haven't reviewed salaries
2 get back to me
3 we haven't had to make
4 are there any other staff developments
5 your department
6 I'm worried about the number of hours

a is particularly vulnerable
b on the horizon?
c for over a year
d any staff redundant
e some of your staff are working
f with recommendations

Words you need

to contain unter Kontrolle bringen
on the horizon in Sicht
touch wood wenn alles gut geht
vulnerable gefährdet

Now look at Liam's notes from the meeting and correct them where necessary.

The Board ~~needs to agree~~ has agreed to a ~~5.5%~~ 5% review, effective from 1 October.
I told Julie that there are at least six staff who should get more than 5% (those who relocated from Canada last year).
Performance review and salary review will be separated in future.

Tell staff
- *There won't be any redundancies this year.*
- *Performance reviews will take place in the new year.*
- *Flexitime will be introduced next year.*
- *No figure for next year's bonuses yet.*

Action
- *Give Julie my recommendations asap.*
- *Keep reviews to the agreed level if possible.*

Can you remember the words Julie and Liam used to talk about changes? Complete the table. Then listen again or read the transcript on page 69 to check. Try to add some words to each column.

Upward movement	Downward movement
an increase	

11 How do you say these figures? Say them or write them out in words, and then check your answers by looking at the box on page 50.

1 €5,000
2 £60,000 pa
3 $50,239,150
4 €70 bn
5 $110,000,000
6 £150 ph

In British English a salary increase is also called a "rise" or "increase". It's called a "raise" in American English.

Talking about figures and numbers

Figures and numbers are used extensively in human resources to talk about salaries, bonuses, and budgets. The following abbreviations are commonly used in writing:

k	thousand	€50 k *(fifty thousand euros)*
m	million	$10 m *(ten million dollars)*
bn	billion	£5.75 bn *(five point seven five billion pounds)*
inc	including	€25,000, inc benefits *(twenty-five thousand euros, including benefits)*
ph	per hour	€10.00 ph *(ten euros per hour)*
pa	per annum	€20,000 pa *(twenty thousand euros per year / per annum)*

Remember

- a *billion* in English means *Milliarde* in German
- we say *two million* or *ten billion* (**not** ~~*two millions*~~ / ~~*ten billions*~~)
- use a point (.) to separate decimals and a comma (,) to separate thousands and millions
- the currency symbol always comes before the number

12 **Match the salaries or wages (1–6) with the extracts from job adverts (a–f) from British job sites.**

1 Salary approx. £28,000 pa
2 £55,724 – £58,750 pa and a relocation package is available
3 £10.50 per inspection
4 £9.25 per hour (rising to £10.50 per hour after 12 weeks)
5 £15.00 ph Monday to Saturday / £18.30 ph Sunday and bank holidays
6 Salary £70,000 + car + extensive benefits

a **Vehicle Inspectors**
Examine the vehicles of prospective insurance customers and complete a simple checklist. Pay according to how many inspections you carry out. Ideal candidate must have own car, hold a full driving license …

b **Customer Service Assistants**
We are currently seeking people with previous customer service experience who can work flexible shifts. The job involves dealing with our customers at the airport, giving advice, recommending products, and offering travel tips …

c **Now recruiting bus drivers …**
Full-time vacancies available for PCV license holders. You will benefit from four weeks' paid holiday, pension plan, and free travel on bus and underground services …

d **Head of HR Department**
One of the oldest police forces in the country with approximately 2,300 staff and an excellent reputation for performance seeks an experienced HR professional to lead a dynamic team …

e **Electricians**
Productivity bonus, 40 hours per week, vehicle supplied. Looking for experienced and qualified electricians to join our busy team. Please request an application by phoning …

f **UK Sales Manager, Essex**
Required to lead the UK sales force. At least five years' successful experience in a similar post in the food and beverage sector is a must.
Excellent communication skills, a flair for business, and a competitive spirit are essential …

How do these salaries and hourly rates compare to those in your country? Discuss with a partner.

Companies Offer Flexible Packages to Entice Best in Field

New research has revealed that many employees don't appreciate their benefits or know their value in monetary terms, despite the fact that 90% of employers believe such benefits are essential to attract and retain high-quality staff.

At a time of strong competition in the recruitment market, it's essential that money is spent on relevant benefits which are appreciated by the employees. There is currently a movement towards more flexible benefits where employees can choose their package, the report stated. Various initiatives are currently being piloted by several major companies.

One company recently decided to introduce a new benefits package in stages, and then issued an employee benefits statement so employees could see exactly what they were getting. Now the company is running focus groups on the plan, with the aim of eventually introducing fully flexible benefits. These focus groups will allow staff and employers to examine the full extent of the benefits being offered, and to find out which benefits present the most value to each individual and how they can best improve the work/life balance of today's employees.

Another company is running its entire benefits program online. Employees are choosing their benefits through the company intranet, and later receive an automatic survey on their satisfaction with the benefits. The HR department can update the benefits offerings on an ongoing basis, and employees can read complete details about their benefits at the click of a mouse.

As long as budgets are not exceeded, what could be better than consulting with employees on what benefits they prefer? If employee satisfaction and productivity continue to rise, flexible benefits may turn out to be the new standard.

Words you need

to appreciate sth. etw. zu schätzen wissen
in monetary terms im finanziellen Sinne
to reveal aufzeigen
stage Etappe
survey Umfrage

Over to you

- Which benefits, if any, are negotiable in your company?
- Which benefits do you consider to be as essential as an employee's salary? Why?
- If flexible benefits packages were offered, how would you go about informing employees so that they make the best decisions?

In this unit you will …
- practice describing union activity
- review the language of negotiations
- practice persuading and bargaining
- read about the future of trade unions

6 Labor Relations

How much do you know about trade unions? Discuss the statements with a partner and correct any that you think are false.

1 Trade unions are called *labor unions* in the US.
2 The largest union in Germany is ver.di.
3 A *closed shop* is common in some large industrial sectors in the UK. It's illegal in Germany.
4 Sweden's Trade Union Confederation represents more than 15% of the country's population – 1.5 million members.
5 The umbrella organization for all German unions is the DGB, Deutscher Gewerkschaftsbund.
6 South Africa has one of the world's lowest rates of industrial action.

"Closed shop" (gewerkschaftspflichtiger Betrieb) means a company can hire only employees who belong to the union.

1 What do you think the headlines are about? Compare your answers with a partner.

Flights Will Resume Immediately Following Ruling Against Pilots

When the Rich Get Richer, Workers Get Organized

Underground Employees Threaten to Take to the Streets

Read the summaries of the three stories behind the headlines to see if you were right.

1 A strike by over 5,000 pilots was recently said to be unlawful by a German labor court, forcing the pilots back to work. Because the pilots were trying to stop the growth of one of the airline's subsidiaries – in addition to demanding increased pay for themselves – the action could not continue, the judge said.
2 Industrial sectors in the US are threatening to strike in a bid for higher wages and improved working conditions. Union leaders are also meeting to negotiate a new collective agreement for autoworkers, the first in a decade. This new union activity comes in response to growing income inequality, as middle-class wages continue to stagnate and executive salaries skyrocket.
3 Following the introduction of an all-night metro service, the union may decide to take industrial action. Union leaders are demanding an above-inflation pay hike and improved safety levels. They claim that poor service will result if wages and conditions are not improved. The metro authority has not yet put forward a counteroffer.

Now find the words in the stories that match the synonyms (a–d).

a attempting ☐☐ ☐ ☐☐☐
b to stop developing to ☐☐☐☐☐☐☐☐
c illegal ☐☐☐☐☐☐☐☐
d increase ☐☐☐☐

2 Put the words (1–6) into the correct order to form phrases from Exercise 1. Then use the phrases to complete the sentences (a–f).

1 action | industrial | take
2 wages | if | not | are | improved | conditions | and
3 to | the | back | pilots | work | forcing
4 increased | demanding | pay
5 for | in | wages | bid | higher | a
6 agreement | a | collective | new | negotiate

a Union representatives have made clear that a strike will happen ....
b Each year we have to .... with the union representatives.
c The workers threatened to .... if the redundancies were carried out.
d Employees have decided to strike .... and improved safety measures in the workplace.
e Following a boost in earnings reported by the company, the principal trade unions are ....
f A decision by the federal court has stopped the strike, ...

Did you know?

Non-union companies in the UK and in the US do not have an official or a recognized joint employee consultation system like the German *Betriebsrat* (works council). Unionized companies have *shop stewards* (also called *union representatives* or *union stewards*) who have been elected by union members to represent them to management. Thus they are a sort of combination of German works council members and trade union negotiators.

3 16 **Listen to a conversation between Jan Weber, the HR manager of a global company in Cologne, and Kevin Linklater, the industrial relations manager of their plant in the UK.**

Which statement in each group best describes the situation they are discussing?

1	a	A 3% increase has been turned down.
	b	A 5% increase has been agreed.
	c	A 5% review was carried out a year ago.
2	a	There may have to be some redundancies worldwide.
	b	There may have to be some redundancies in the UK.
	c	There may have to be some redundancies in Amsterdam.
3	a	White-collar staff have had salaries frozen for five years.
	b	White-collar salaries were last reviewed two years ago.
	c	White-collar staff have no chance of a salary review.
4	a	Workers at the plant are on strike.
	b	Workers at the plant are dissatisfied with the proposed wage increase.
	c	Workers at the plant are concerned about safety issues.
5	a	Workers at the plant have heard rumors of closure.
	b	Workers at the plant have heard rumors that wages may be reduced.
	c	Workers at the plant have heard rumors that jobs may be transferred to Poland.

4 16 **Listen to the dialogue again and complete the questions with the words in the box. Then use the information in the dialogue to answer the questions.**

agreement • behind • counterargument • fail • freeze • rumors • tactics

1 What's .... the union's rejection of the pay deal?

2 What exactly was Kevin's ....?

3 Why did the union representatives and their members .... to reach an ....?

4 Why did they .... the salaries of white-collar staff two years ago?

5 What are the .... going around the plant?

6 Why have Jan and Kevin got to plan their ....?

It looks as if there could be a long and difficult negotiation with the union representing the workers at the British plant. How can companies avoid situations like this? Discuss with a partner.

5 **Which phrase in each pair matches the definition (1–6)?**

1 to reject a proposal or suggestion
  a to make a counteroffer
  b to fail to reach agreement

2 workers on the production line
  a blue-collar workers
  b white-collar workers

3 a general fall in orders across many business sectors
  a when productivity is down
  b an economic downturn

4 a response to another suggestion
  a a counterargument
  b a negotiation

5 the place where the goods are produced
  a the plant
  b the shop floor

6 to stop pay for a certain period
  a to freeze salaries
  b to negotiate a new pay deal

6 **What makes a successful negotiation? Work with a partner to rank the tips below from 1 to 10 (1 = most important). Can you add any more tips to the list?**

- Always listen carefully to the other person.
- Be flexible and prepared to compromise.
- Be positive – highlight common ground.
- Build rapport and be courteous.
- Use simple and clear language.
- Use persuasion, not threats.
- Prepare your arguments.
- Be constructive and avoid open conflict.
- Always remember your aims.
- When agreement is reached, summarize clearly and close the deal.

7 **Match the sentences below (1–10) to the five parts of a negotiation. Check your answers with a partner.**

building rapport
establishing objectives and aims
bargaining
addressing conflict
concluding

1 Excellent, then let me close by summing up what we've agreed on.
2 If the white-collar workers accepted a pay freeze last year, it's not unreasonable to give them a higher increase now.
3 Let's not get too hot under the collar.
4 We'd like to start by welcoming everyone and restating our proposals.
5 Believe me, we'd really like to shake hands and walk out of here today with a deal.
6 But we want your assurances that there will be no industrial action.
7 We are happy to meet you today to work out a solution.
8 That's it, then. A successful conclusion for everybody.
9 We've studied the figures, and the bottom line is that there's not much money in the pot, so we simply have to reach a compromise.
10 Management has asked us to give you their assurances on this point.

8 **Form collocations used in negotiations by matching the verbs (1–8) with the nouns (a–h) and the correct definitions (A–H).**

verbs
1 to work out
2 to reject
3 to contain
4 to threaten
5 to face
6 to reach
7 to put
8 to post

nouns
a a compromise
b something on the notice board
c closure
d the offer
e costs
f a solution
g industrial action
h your cards on the table

definitions
A to refuse a suggestion
B to say you intend to strike
C to agree to meet in the middle
D to confront the possibility of shutting down (part of the company)
E to solve by reasoning
F to hold expenses within a fixed limit
G to speak openly about one's position
H to display information for everyone in the company to read

17 **Check your answers by listening to Kevin Linklater and Jan Weber negotiating with the union representatives, Katherine White and Paul Ashton.**

Words you need

closure Schließung
hot under the collar wütend
to take effect in Kraft treten
threat / to threaten Drohung / drohen

Now decide whether the statements about the negotiation are true or false.

	True	False
1 Things will get worse in the next six to nine months, as the economic outlook is worsening.		
2 Overtime is only allowed on the night shift.		
3 If the workers don't get more money, they will go on strike.		
4 The area where the plant is located has high unemployment.		
5 The management can't promise anything positive.		
6 Sales have been getting worse in the Netherlands.		

9 After the meeting, Kevin writes an email to the management committee. Complete the gaps with the correct form of the verbs in the box.

accept · be · give · meet · not be (2x) · receive · transfer

Dear Management Committee,

As you know, Jan Weber and I ....[1] with the union representatives last night to discuss their rejection of the pay offer of 3%, effective 1 March and the threat of industrial action. Apart from being aware that white-collar workers ....[2] 5%, there ....[3], as I suspected, strong rumors going round that we're closing the plant and ....[4] work to Poland.

We ....[5] the union representatives our assurances that this ....[6] the case and agreed the 3% increase from 1 March, followed by a further 1.5% in nine months, as long as there ....[7] a substantial fall in sales and provided that there is no industrial action. They ....[8] the offer on behalf of their members.

We feel this is a successful conclusion to the negotiations.

Best wishes,
Kevin Linklater

What types of negotiations have you been involved in? Describe your experiences to your colleagues.

The language of negotiating

A negotiation is often a very delicate procedure where even the language you use can influence the outcome. While diplomatic language (see page 39) and building rapport are both essential for keeping the negotiation polite, there are also many fixed phrases which can help make finding the right words easier. Below are some typical phrases for persuading and bargaining.

Persuading
- It would be to your advantage to ...
- It might be in your interest to ...
- We can reassure you on that point totally.
- It's the best offer around. You won't find a better one.

Bargaining
- We would agree on one condition.
- If you agree to ..., we can ...
- If you threaten to strike, we'll withdraw the offer.
- If you stopped picketing, then I think we could make a counteroffer.
- We might put a better offer on the table, provided (that) you stop the strike.
- I'd go along with that on the condition that you returned to work.
- That seems to be a good compromise, as long as there is no industrial action of any kind.
- Unless your members return to work tomorrow, we'll withdraw our offer.

10 **Use the key words in brackets to make complete sentences about the conditions and offers.**

1 our members get 5% increase in pay / take industrial action (*unless/will*)
Unless our members get a 5% increase in pay, they will take industrial action.
2 be an increase in sales / offer a further 2% pay rise (*provided/can*)
3 no further increases in pay / be no job losses Amsterdam (*if/will*)
4 another review in nine months / be no industrial action (*will / on condition that*)
5 productivity increased / pay a bonus end of the year (*if/could*)
6 open on Sundays from 10:00 a.m. to 4:00 p.m. / lose business to competitors (*unless/will*)
7 customer service not suffer / introduce flexible working hours (*provided/can*)

11 **Work with a partner. Choose a few situations below – or think of your own – and try to persuade your partner to accept your position. Be prepared to bargain.**

1 You've referred several people for a personal assistant position. You feel that one candidate is clearly the best, but the manager prefers another person.
2 You need two staff to work on the weekend.
3 You'd like to take three of your six weeks' holiday together this year. (The rule is a maximum of two weeks at a time.)
4 Your back office now needs to work a two-shift day: 5:00 a.m. – 1:00 p.m. and 1:00 p.m. – 9:00 p.m. The staff are not happy about this.
5 An employee has decided to leave the company. You need to convince him/her to stay.

12 **Complete the sentences with words related to the root words. You might need to add prefixes or suffixes and change the form.**

negotiate	1 Kevin Linklater has an excellent record as a first-class .... 2 The offer we made to the union was non-.................... . 3 The next .... on pay and conditions takes place on Tuesday, September 1.
consult	4 When we have a tough problem with the union, we use a .... from a firm of industrial mediators. 5 Our joint .... committee meets twice a year. 6 .... with the union can be difficult even at the best of times!

13 **Work with a partner to do a role-play. First look at the tips and the phrases in this unit. Then use the role cards in the Partner Files or think up your own situation to negotiate on with your partner.**

> Partner File 6: Partner A, page 62 / Partner B, page 65

The Future of Trade Unions

What will trade unions look like in 20, 50, or 100 years? Simon Mitchell, a London-based consultant, predicts the future for organized labor.

The role of trade unions has changed considerably in the last decades. Global competition, outsourcing, new government regulations, and other factors have caused a significant fall in union membership.

In order to stay relevant, union leaders and their members need to review their goals and revise their methods. Here are some new directions that trade unions might go in the 21st century.

The International Union
We often hear complaints about global competition and losing jobs to foreign workers. Outsourcing is an irreversible trend, but that doesn't mean unions don't have a role – they simply have to change their perspective. How can you incorporate those foreign workers into your organization? How can Brazilian and German steel workers collaborate to better the working conditions in both countries? Unions will need to be global players in order to get meaningful results.

The Digital Union
Labor unions can no longer drag their feet when it comes to using new technologies to communicate with their members. On the contrary, unions will have to embrace the Internet, and social media in particular, in order to stay effective and relevant. New technologies will serve two main purposes: 1) to engage the next generation of workers, "digital natives" who grew up with computers, and 2) to find new ways to reduce costs through technology, for example by informing and organizing members through free online services.

Advocating Skills Instead of Benefits
As the 21st century has already shown us, modern workers need to be as dynamic and flexible as the companies they work for. Unions need to accept and understand this fact, and encourage their members to constantly develop new skills and learn new technologies. From now on, the best job security will be a willingness to adapt and grow.

Better Branding
The term *organized labor* just isn't very exciting nowadays, is it? Union leaders will have to build a new identity for their organizations – an identity that's positive, evolving, human, and energetic. The best way to accomplish this will be to highlight the invaluable role that unions play in society by stabilizing the economy, building a strong middle class, resolving disputes, and creating paths toward success for their members.

Words you need

considerably wesentlich
to drag one's feet hinterherhinken
on the contrary im Gegenteil
to revise revidieren, überarbeiten

Over to you

- Do you agree with the author of this article that unions will need to change the way they operate in order to survive in the future?
- Are there other ways that you think unions will have to evolve in order to stay relevant and effective?
- In your experience, what are the one or two major factors that are preventing labor organizations from better achieving their goals?

Partner Files

Partner A

Unit 1

Exercise 14 • File 1

▷ p. 12

You're an HR manager working in the corporate headquarters of an international company. You're visiting one of your European branches and are meeting with Partner B, who's a manager there, to discuss recruiting a new marketing manager. Note the following points:

- You want to post the position online using several different job sites in order to ensure wide exposure.
- Candidates are expected to have an extensive network of contacts, therefore you think it's also important to advertise the job on a professional social networking platform.
- No one applied for the job when it was advertised internally.

Ask for Partner B's suggestions and give feedback. Try to agree on how you should recruit for this position.

Unit 2

Exercise 9 • File 2

▷ p. 19

You have applied for a job as an administrative assistant at the headquarters of Consolidated Life, and on Monday, 28 August, you receive an email inviting you to an interview. The interview should take place within the next two weeks, and you may also be asked to spend a day at an assessment center. Look at your calendar and your notes, and then call Consolidated Life's office to arrange a time.

Notes for scheduling the interview:
- *Mention vacation Sept. 10–24 (taking children to visit parents) conflicts with assessment center?*
- *Ask for directions to office.*
- *Is parking available?*

August/September

Sunday	Monday	Tuesday	Wednesday	Thursday	Friday	Saturday
27	28 *Mtg.* *2–6 p.m.*	29	30 ←	31 *Project work 6–8 p.m.*	1 →	2
3	4 *Dentist appt.* *4 p.m.*	5 ←	6 *Training course in Reading*	7	8 →	9

▷ p. 30

Exercise 11 • File 3

You are an HR manager at the Austrian subsidiary of Wald-Richter International Books, which is based in Stuttgart. You are currently looking for someone for the position of bookkeeper and are meeting with a candidate – the most qualified one so far – to discuss the terms and conditions of employment. Note that the job requires someone with fluent German (spoken and written) but the company is prepared to pay for German lessons. The applicant lives in Vienna so there is no relocation involved. Use the notes to conduct the interview.

- hours (no flextime)
- vacation time
- sick pay
- benefits
- German language training twice a week

▷ p. 40

Exercise 10 • File 4

You are a recruitment manager in a large HR department and are getting ready for your first performance review with your boss, the director of recruitment.

You've been with the company for one year now (including the six-month probationary period). You started off well in the job and were very happy – it's a challenging post with lots of contact with other branches. In preparation for the performance review, make notes of some of the things you feel you do well and which make you suitable for the position.

Strengths:

1 *Six years' recruiting experience in previous company*
2 *Attention to detail*
3 ....
4 ....

Although you like your job, lately you have been thinking about looking for a new position. The reason is that one of your colleagues (Becker) has been making things unpleasant for you for the last 4–5 months. (He/She comments on your work, removes paperwork from your desk, talks about you behind your back, etc.) You feel like you're in a difficult position and have even been to a doctor for stress-related problems.

Prepare what you want to say, then take part in the performance review with your superior. (He/She talked to you briefly some months ago about your performance, but you decided not to go into detail at that time.) Then swap roles and do the review again.

Unit 5

Exercise 8 • File 5

▷ p. 47

You are one of three HR managers who comprise the remuneration committee. You are meeting to discuss a new benefits package. You have agreed to chair the meeting, so first you need to use the notes from the last meeting to prepare the agenda.

> *Draft agenda*
> - *Most important benefits?*
>   - *a flexible working hours essential*
>   - *b childcare facilities needed to encourage female employees to go back to work*
>   - *c some sort of profit-sharing bonus?*
> - *Conclusions and recommendations (should we look at health and sports club issues?)*

You think flexible working hours are essential, so prepare a list of what you propose exactly (flextime, create part-time jobs, job-sharing in some areas, etc.). You would also like to recommend some sports / health-related benefits; decide what these could be (club memberships, massage, sauna, etc.). Start the meeting by introducing the agenda and then discuss the various benefits that have been recommended with your colleagues. Try to agree on the next steps. (You think you need to go slowly on this – you won't be able to make a decision today. Perhaps you need to first ask the staff what additional benefits they would like to have, meet again, and then make a proposal to the board.)

Unit 6

Exercise 13 • File 6

▷ p. 58

Your company has decided to make five IT staff redundant, as the whole IT operation is being outsourced to an independent contractor.

You are a senior manager in the HR department and are meeting with a member of the works council to get their agreement, which you need in order to go ahead with the plan. Prepare for the meeting by completing the notes below. You might also want to think of some other arguments. (You expect this to be a difficult meeting as you know there have been some bad rumors going around.)

> **Meeting – IT redundancies**
> - cost saving €.................... pa to outsource IT
> - four of the five employees will be offered contracts with the independent contractor
> - the independent contractor offers 24-hour in-house IT service (in place of the current 15-hour coverage)
> - three of the redundant staff have 10–12 years' service and two joined in the last five months (still completing their probationary period – not normally subject to redundancy laws so company is being generous).
> - you will offer the employees the following redundancy settlement:
>   - ► .... month's salary for every year worked
>   - ► additional €.................... bonus if employed for more than .... years

Partner Files

Partner B

▷ p. 12 Exercise 14 • File 1 **Unit 1**

You're the manager of a European branch of an international company. An HR manager from your corporate headquarters (Partner A) is visiting you to discuss recruitment for a marketing manager at your branch office. Note the following points:

- You plan to advertise the job on the careers page of the company intranet.
- In your experience, online professional networks can be time-consuming and aren't taken seriously.
- You know of someone in the company who's a suitable candidate and should be approached directly.

Make suggestions and give feedback on Partner A's suggestions. Try to agree on how you should recruit for this position.

▷ p. 19 Exercise 9 • File 2 **Unit 2**

You are a recruitment specialist at the headquarters of Consolidated Life. You are responsible for arranging and carrying out interviews for the position of administrative assistant. The best candidates have been emailed and will call you to arrange an interview. They may also have to spend a day at an assessment center. Use your notes and this extract from your calendar to handle the phone call and to make an appointment for an interview next week, ideally on either 7 or 8 September. (Today is 28 August.)

Notes for all applicants for administrative assistant position:
- *Should bring application form to interview.*
- *Mention assessment center dates.*
- *Give directions to nearby parking garage.*

August/September

Sunday	Monday	Tuesday	Wednesday	Thursday	Friday	Saturday
27	28	29	30	31 Visit Hamburg office ⟵	1 ⟶	2
3	4 10–12 dept. mtg.	5	6	7 Interviews (assess. center 21st or 26st Sept.) ⟵	8 ⟶	9

Unit 3

Exercise 11 • File 3

▷ p. 30

You have applied for the position of bookkeeper at the Austrian subsidiary of Wald-Richter International Books, which is based in Stuttgart. Wald-Richter is looking for somebody fluent in German to deal with its Austrian clients, and although you have lived in Vienna for three years, you are worried that your German won't be good enough. You are meeting with an HR manager at Wald-Richter to discuss the terms and conditions of the job.

Here are the things to ask about at the interview:

- Flextime? You need to take your seven-year-old child to school each day, so you can't start before 9:30 a.m. The afternoon is no problem, as your partner collects your child from school.
- Two-week vacation has already been planned – will the company allow this?
- Your German is good, but not fluent. Are lessons available?

Unit 4

Exercise 10 • File 4

▷ p. 40

You are the director of recruitment in a large HR department and are about to carry out a performance review with one of your recruitment managers who has completed a year's service. You were very happy with his/her work during the six-month probationary period, but it seems something has gone wrong. You feel he/she has good potential and would like him/her to be a success.

Look at the notes you have made about some problems and prepare some questions to ask the employee during the performance review. Then swap roles and do the review again.

Problems over the last six months:

- *Two periods of sickness of 10 days each. Would he/she like to share more information about this?*
- *A lot of mistakes reported*
- *Complaint from a long-term employee and colleague (Becker) about long breaks from the desk, lack of attention to detail*
- *We spoke briefly three months ago (she/he was nervous and tense)*

▷ p. 47 Exercise 8 • File 5 **Unit 5**

You are one of three HR managers who comprise the remuneration committee. You are meeting to discuss a new benefits package. You have agreed to take the minutes in this second meeting.

- You personally think childcare facilities for both male and female staff are the most essential benefit to offer. (You have two children aged two and six, and your partner is currently on maternity/paternity leave for one year.) So far, only one man has taken paternity leave in your company, and there are a number of female colleagues who are under extreme stress because they can't find reliable childcare they can afford.
- You don't think bonuses are a good idea; most people prefer to have a good salary and a better work/life balance.

You feel there has now been enough discussion (and you are very busy with other things at the moment), so you want to make a decision quickly! Prepare some suggestions for resolving the childcare issues to present at the meeting and try to agree with your colleagues on the next steps.

▷ p. 58 Exercise 13 • File 6 **Unit 6**

You are a member of the works council. You have a negotiation meeting with a senior HR manager about five redundancies in the IT department. As far as you know, the five employees are being made redundant without good reason (it seems the company wants to outsource the jobs to an independent contractor) and you've heard the company isn't being very generous with its redundancy settlement. Check your notes before going into the negotiation and try to add one or two other points to negotiate.

Points to raise at meeting:

- *Over the last two years, 10 key staff have been outsourced to different companies. We need some assurances this will not continue.*
- *What compensation payment is the company proposing to pay redundant employees? (Negotiate a higher one!)*
- *The company says it is saving costs by outsourcing. What will the money saved be used for? Who will benefit?*

Partner C

▷ p. 47 Exercise 8 • File 5 **Unit 5**

You are one of three HR managers who comprise the remuneration committee. You are meeting to discuss a new benefits package.

Childcare issues are fine, but you don't have children and would prefer to have some sort of reward incentives (profit-sharing, performance-related pay, free shares in the company, etc.) which would motivate all employees, not just those with children. You agree that some sort of flexible working arrangements are necessary, though – too many of your colleagues work excessive overtime, and there have been one or two cases of stress-related illnesses recently.

Decide what recommendations you would like to make exactly, and be ready to present your suggestions at the meeting. Hopefully you and your colleagues can agree on a proposal today so you can make recommendations to the board this week. (You have offered to write the email to the board stating the committee's proposals and you are going on a two-week holiday in three days.)

Transcripts

Unit 1 Exercise 8

02

Lisa Good morning, Robert. How was your weekend?

Robert Excellent, thanks. Too short, though!

Lisa Yes, I know what you mean. Do you have a moment?

Robert Sure, what's up?

Lisa I just wanted to have a word with you about the search for an HR manager in Berlin. Could you give me an update?

Robert Well, the job description and person specification have both been finalized, and Thomas Scholz in Berlin has signed off on them. We're looking for someone with two-to-five years' generalist HR experience, either an HR qualification or a degree, and, of course, they must be highly proficient in English.

Lisa Where are you planning to advertise?

Robert Well, firstly on the company intranet, on the European careers page, although I don't think there's much chance of finding an internal candidate.

Lisa I'm not sure I agree with you there. Don't forget we took on a lot of employees with the merger two years ago – there might be some HR potential there.

Robert Thanks, that's a great point. I'm also going to post the position on the careers page of our website, where we list all new openings, and on a couple of job sites which operate internationally.

Lisa OK, sounds good. By the way, I believe there's a German trade journal for HR professionals. You might look into that, too.

Robert Ah, I'm one step ahead of you! I've already looked into it. It's a well-respected magazine, but their circulation is actually quite limited, and their advertising rates are high.

Lisa OK, thanks. I should have known you'd be on top of things! So, where are you going to hold the interviews?

Robert Well, I thought I'd offer interviews in both our UK and our Berlin offices, if that's OK. It's important that Thomas Scholz is involved. As the general manager, he and the recruitment manager will need to work together closely on the future recruitment campaign in Berlin.

Lisa Yes, good idea. Well, Robert, you clearly have things under control. Keep me posted as you move forward.

Robert No problem, will do.

Lisa All right, thanks. I've got to run now, actually. I have a meeting about disciplinary procedures in about five minutes, and then I'll be out of the office. But I'll be back again on Thursday, so perhaps we can talk again then.

Unit 2 Exercise 8

03

Liz NewMobile Ltd., Liz Winston speaking.

Caroline Good morning. My name is Caroline Dugard and I'm phoning about an interview for the position of call center team leader. I was asked to phone you to arrange a time.

Liz Good morning, Caroline. Let me just get your file. Here it is. So, can you come by to see us for an initial interview next week?

Caroline Unfortunately, that won't be possible. I'm going to be in Chicago next week on business. I could come the week after that, though.

Liz Yes, that's fine. No problem. So, let's see, can you come in on Wednesday the 10th at 4:00 p.m.?

Caroline Could you just remind me exactly where your office is?

Liz Of course. We're in Midtown on 43rd Street, right by Grand Central Station.

Caroline Right, well that's fine then. I could come in that day, but could we make it a little later, perhaps at 4:30 p.m.?

Liz Yes, let's say 4:30 p.m., then.

Caroline That's great, thank you. By the way, the application form wasn't attached to the email.

Liz I'm sorry about that. I'll email it over to you now. You can fill it out at home and bring it along with you to the interview.

Caroline Great. Oh, and one last thing. Would you be able to let me know who I'll be meeting with?

Liz Sure thing. I don't have that information in front of me right now, but I'll let you know when I email you the application form.

Caroline Thanks very much.

Liz My pleasure. We look forward to meeting you.

Caroline Likewise. Goodbye.

Liz Bye.

Unit 2 Exercise 11

Part 1 04

Heather I think that fills you in on the job requirements. So, could you tell me about your experience as a team leader in your present job?

Caroline Yes, I've been in my present job for five years. I started as an associate in the call center, and was promoted to team leader two years ago. I'm one of eight team leaders and we cover two shifts, seven days a week.

Heather What exactly does that involve?

Caroline Well, I'm responsible for 10 call center associates, and I report to the call center supervisor. We handle a wide variety of customer needs every day, and I assist the associates whenever they encounter a difficult situation. As you can see from my resume, I also did customer service in a production company for six years before that.

Part 2 05

Heather Could you outline some of the problems you've dealt with as a team leader?

Caroline Well, they relate mainly to difficult customers and to one or two personality conflicts within the call center team.

Heather Could you expand on that a little more?

Caroline When a problem arises between staff members on the same team, then we usually resolve it by moving one person to another team. Team leaders meet weekly to discuss the overall situation, and we operate a very flexible call center where the staff move around to different sections frequently to gain more experience.

Heather And how do you deal with difficult customers, or with customers who have a complaint?

Caroline We have a policy in our call center which says that a difficult or dissatisfied customer should be transferred to a team leader immediately. It's one of our specific responsibilities. Otherwise my staff are instructed to tell customers that I'll call them back as soon as possible. If I'm not there, then another team leader handles the situation.

Part 3 06

Heather What aspect of your job do you like best, Caroline?

Caroline I particularly enjoy dealing with customers. I have the ability to build a good rapport with people on the telephone. It's something that comes naturally to me.

Heather Why do you want to leave your present job?

Caroline Part of the call center is being relocated. My partner has a good job in this area and we have two children at school. I don't really want to move at this time, although my company has asked me if I would like to relocate.

Heather I see. Thank you. As you know, the next part of the interview process would be an assessment center.

Unit 3 Exercise 2

07

Nancy Hi, Laura, thanks for coming in today. I'm glad we could arrange a time to meet.

Laura My pleasure. It was really exciting to be offered the position, and I'm looking forward to getting started.

Nancy Great. Well, we'd like to tell you about the conditions of employment. Of course, this information will also be in the contract of employment and the company handbook, as well as in the offer letter.

Gabe That's right. And you might find some employment procedures are different from those in Germany, but we offer very good terms, I think. As we go through the contract, please feel free to ask about anything you're not sure of.

Laura OK, thanks.

Nancy Right. Let's start with your hours. We have a standard 40-hour work week, with normal working hours being nine to six, Monday to Friday, including an hour for lunch. I'm afraid we don't offer flexitime yet, and there may be overtime during busy periods. This is either paid or given as time off in lieu.

Laura I see. Could you just explain what you mean by *in lieu*?

Nancy Sure, that just means you'll be given the equivalent in time off for those extra hours worked.

Laura Ah, I see.

Gabe By the way, we're currently looking at more flexible working arrangements for our employees, but that's still in the future.

Laura OK. Could you tell me what happens if I get sick?

Nancy Sure. Our policy is that we pay for the first 12 weeks of illness, and after that, we have an insurance plan which would continue to pay you.

Gabe Yes, and if you're ill, we expect you to let us know as early as possible, and then to keep us informed after that.

Laura Of course, that all makes sense. Now, would you mind telling me about vacation time?

Nancy Your annual holiday entitlement is 20 days, which rises to 25 after two years. Before taking any time off, the dates need to be cleared with your department head, of course.

Laura Well, there is something I did want to mention. I already have a week's vacation booked in two months' time – will this be an issue?

Gabe I'm sure that won't be an issue, as it's only a week. But we can discuss that in detail later.

Laura Great. Well, that all sounds very straightforward. When will it be possible to see the contract?

Nancy We don't have the final version with us now, but it will be sent as an attachment with the offer letter, which you'll receive by email.

Gabe Now, about references. I wanted to let you know that we'll be contacting your previous and current employers. I believe in Germany you normally include references with your application, but here in the UK we prefer to request references ourselves, which is why the offer of employment is subject to satisfactory references.

Laura Yes, I understand. That's no problem. I've given the details for all my references on the application form. My present employer in Hamburg knows I'm leaving, so you can go ahead and contact my supervisor. I'll tell her to expect to hear from you.

Gabe Well thanks, Laura. I hope you'll be joining us soon and I look forward to welcoming you to the department. Maybe you'd like to get to know the team over lunch? We'll be going to the canteen in around 15 minutes.

Laura That sounds nice, thanks.

Unit 3 **Exercise 12**

08

Even in the best-run companies, there are many internal problems that can occur. Frequent issues faced by HR departments include sexual harassment, bullying, health and safety issues, terms or conditions, management decisions, as well as discrimination – for example, on the grounds of race, gender, sexual identification, disability, or religion.

When someone starts in a new position, he or she is entitled to a written statement laying out the main conditions of their employment. As well as information on pay, hours, paid vacation, and the benefits package, the statement must also cover what the company will do if they have to discipline an employee for breaking the rules, which is called the warning procedure. This statement should also make clear who the employee can appeal to if they are dissatisfied with a disciplinary decision. All employees have the right to be accompanied by another employee or a union representative, if applicable, to any disciplinary meeting or hearing.

A disciplinary procedure is normally started when an employee does not follow company policy, breaks rules, or displays inappropriate workplace behavior. Employees must be fully informed of their inappropriate behavior and given an opportunity to explain themselves. The procedure should be handled in a private and respectful manner, and the employee's previous record should be taken into account.

Unit 4 **Exercise 2**

09

1

Because we are a multinational corporation and our business approaches have to function globally, I recommend that we introduce team development training for our managers, and also for our staff generally. My proposal is to put it on the agenda for the international managers meeting in three weeks' time.

10

2

It's essential that we enable our employees to broaden their professional skills and keep up-to-date in their field of work. We'll lose staff if we continue to expect them to muddle through without investing in their – and our – future!

11

3

Clearly this should be dealt with by the manager personally. It's high time we introduced a performance review program. This is long overdue and will focus managers' minds on the development and evaluation of their employees and hopefully avoid a lot of communication problems like this one.

12

4

In order to avoid problems like this, we need to introduce an induction program to inform and empower new employees. Maybe we should also look into the benefits of a mentoring scheme, too.

Unit 4 **Exercise 6**

13

Jordan Well, my biggest strengths are paying attention to detail and accuracy. Unfortunately, this slows me down and sometimes things get a little behind.

Anna How do you see the relationship with your team?

Jordan OK. I don't seem to have any problems there.

Anna And the output of your team? Tell me about that.

Jordan Well, we were on target for the first three months of the year, and then we fell behind because of staff difficulties.

Anna To be quite frank, Jordan, you were actually down 25% for six months of the year.

Jordan Yes, well, that's because Marco was on sick leave for so long.

Anna I see. When did you realize that his absence would cause problems with meeting targets?

Jordan Well, I knew it would from the beginning.

Anna Then could you tell me why you didn't come to see me, Jordan?

Jordan You were away on that project in Turkey, and I'd hoped to solve the problem myself by working overtime. And with the help of Lara Hoff.

Anna So what happened then? Why didn't it work?

Jordan Lara had family business to take care of at home, so she couldn't put in extra time, and I had too much to do with the day-to-day stuff. No one else was able to do it.

Anna With respect, I was only away for a month. Why didn't you raise this issue at the regular team meetings?

Jordan Well, I just prefer to deal with these things myself. And besides, you're always busy.

Anna But the results are not very impressive, Jordan. Your team can't help to resolve the problems if you don't discuss them. We have meetings in order to delegate work and find creative solutions to issues like these. So, how do you suggest we go on? How can I help you?

Jordan Well, perhaps we could have another team member until Marco returns, and maybe I need some training in leadership skills and time management. Actually, there's a bit of a cultural problem with Marco, too. Before he was out sick, he was having difficulty dealing with the Austrian formality and wasn't very happy here. That caused a few problems with other members of the team.

Anna Well, neither of the first two suggestions should present a problem. I'll talk to our production director this afternoon. And I know about Marco's problems. He has discussed them with me and we're sending him on some cultural training when he is back. We may do it for all of your team as it's such a mixed group. But, I'd like to add one more thing: I think you and I need to check in with each other more often, so let's meet weekly for a while and see how it goes. OK?

Jordan OK. That sounds good.

Anna Right. Going back to the question of output, we have to get your team's output up to scratch as soon as possible. I'd like you to arrange a meeting with your team and discuss how you can improve performance in the coming months. OK?

Jordan Yes, fine.

Anna Finally, on a personal note, Jordan, how is your wife settling in? I think there were a few problems initially?

Jordan Yes, that's right. Actually, she's now found a job in her field – she's a physiotherapist – and she's very happy with it. So that has taken a lot of worry off my shoulders.

Unit 5 Exercise 2

14

Julie As you know, we need to review our benefits package. We've received some suggestions from our colleagues in the Netherlands, but we have to see if these suggestions match our needs here. What's your view on this? Natalia?

Natalia I've been reviewing the suggestions from our Amsterdam office. They make some good points, and I have some ideas of my own, too. For example, I think we need to introduce more family-friendly benefits. Too many staff are working overtime and having problems with their work/life balance.

Julie Hmm, OK. Could I have your input, Alex?

Alex Well, what exactly do you mean by family-friendly benefits, Natalia?

Natalia I was thinking of parental leave in particular, but also flexible working hours.

Alex Well, I'm definitely in favor of flexible working hours. However, I think we should also look closely at childcare services to encourage our staff to come back to work after taking parental leave. In fact I'd like to submit a proposal on this at a future meeting.

Julie Good idea. How much time do you need? Could you submit something at our regular meeting on the 15th?

Alex Sure, no problem.

Julie Great. And Natalia, could you please prepare a summary of all our current benefits and ask accounting to print off a list of the annual costs? I want to look at overall costs, and also see a breakdown of how much we're spending in each benefit category.

Natalia OK. By the way, I've also done research on new initiatives for flexible working, so I'll fill you in on that, too.

Julie Good. And I'll give you the details of the new profit-sharing bonus the directors have been discussing.

Unit 5 Exercise 10

15

Julie Well, Liam, as you know, we haven't reviewed salaries for over a year. The board has agreed on a maximum 5% increase from the 1st of October, and I'd like you to get back to me with recommendations for all your staff. Here's a list with the relevant data about each employee in Marketing.

Liam That's fine, I've got one or two people who deserve more than 5%, particularly those who came from London and New York last year. They actually took a drop in salary, and they've reminded me about this several times. It's been 18 months since we had our last raise, too.

Julie Well, we might be able to give more in one or two cases if you reward less in others. Don't forget the rate of inflation is not expected to rise much in Britain this year, and so far, touch wood, we haven't had to make any staff redundant.

Liam What's the situation likely to be on the bonuses at the end of the year? Will they be cut? And are there any other staff developments on the horizon?

Julie Well, we're proposing to carry out the performance reviews in November and early December, and that will determine the final bonus amounts. We're aiming to separate the salary review from the performance review in the future. We're also looking at the issues of flexible working and childcare. Your department is particularly vulnerable here, as you have less staff and a number of them are working too many hours. Also, there are several women on maternity leave at present who I believe you would like back. Frankly, Liam, I'm worried about the number of hours some of your staff are working. It has to be contained.

Liam OK, I hope we'll have the opportunity of discussing some of these issues at the management meeting. Thanks, Julie. I'll get back to you within a week.

Unit 6 Exercise 3

16

Kevin I'm afraid we've got a problem, Jan. The 3% increase that management agreed to for the plant has been rejected by the union.

Jan Oh, no. What's the story?

Kevin They want the same increase as the white-collar staff – at least 5%. The union representatives held a meeting with their members last night and failed to reach agreement.

Jan What was your counterargument?

Kevin We haven't had an official meeting yet – that will be next week. But I told them that sales were down and that if things got worse, we might have to think about some redundancies in Amsterdam. I also reminded them that they had a 3% review a year ago.

Jan Did you know that the white-collar staff haven't had a review in salary for two years now? We froze their salaries because we'd lost a huge contract, and then there was a recession, but we decided to review the shop-floor workers to avoid industrial action. All this happened just before you joined.

Kevin I see. Well, I know they want at least 5%. It appears there have been rumors of an economic downturn in the industry and the transfer of work to the Polish subsidiary. So of course the staff are nervous about the future of the plant. Despite this, they still feel 3% is too low and doesn't compensate them for loss of overtime over the last six months.

Jan It's not really a fair demand. But to be honest, I expected this would happen.

Kevin We've got to plan our tactics. We can't offer 5%, that's for sure, but we don't want any strikes at present. Let's talk to the management committee again before the meeting.

Unit 6 Exercise 8

17

Kevin Thank you for calling the meeting. We're happy to have the chance to speak with you today, and to try to work out a solution. We'd like to start by welcoming everyone and restating our proposals. Then perhaps you could outline why the offer was rejected by your members. Jan, would you like to begin?

Jan Yes. A 3% increase has been agreed to, which we consider is a reasonable and fair offer given the current economic situation and the fact that our sales are down. The outlook isn't a very bright one at present, but we think things will improve in the next six to nine months provided we can contain costs. I'd also like to remind you that you had a 3% review a year ago while the salaries of the white-collar workers were frozen.

Katherine But our members aren't happy with 3% and, since overtime was stopped six months ago, they feel they have suffered enough. It's a difficult situation, that's true, but they want a minimum of 5%. What's more, they are threatening industrial action if they don't get it.

Kevin That's a bit unfair, isn't it? I heard there are some rumors going around about transferring work to a Polish subsidiary. Has this got anything to do with it?

Paul Yes, that's right. They are worried that the plant is facing closure. That would be a disaster for an area like this, which is already facing high unemployment. You know what rumors are like.

Jan We'd like to reassure you that, as far as we're aware, there is no plan to close the plant or transfer business out of the country. Management has asked us to give you their assurances on this point. We've studied the figures, and the bottom line is that there is not much money in the pot, so we simply have to reach a compromise

Paul I'm sorry, but why should we believe this? Outsourcing is happening everywhere at present – cheaper labor, cheaper factories …

Kevin Let's not get too hot under the collar, Paul. We consider ourselves to be a fair and reasonable employer with a consistent record of commitment and honesty with our employees. There's also the Dutch plant to consider. As I mentioned when we met before, if sales continue to fall in Amsterdam, we'll have a big problem here. We think we can deal with it, but if we have to pay out more money here, then it's unlikely we can. Listen, we'd like to put our cards on the table. If your members accept 3% now, we will give a further one and a half percent in nine months, as long as there isn't a substantial drop in sales. But we want your assurances that there will be no industrial action.

Katherine Could we have 10 minutes to talk about it outside?

Kevin Certainly. Let's break for coffee and meet back in 20 minutes …

. . .

Katherine OK. We think this is a reasonable compromise. Our members will agree to 3% now and one and a half percent in nine months. And you have our assurances there will be no industrial action.

Jan That's it then. A successful conclusion for everybody. Thank you.

Kevin Good, I'll send you written confirmation tomorrow, which you can post on the notice boards on the shop floor if you like. The 3% review will take effect from the 1st of March.

Answer Key

Unit 1

Warmer
(suggested answers)
2 a 3 c 4 d 5 g 6 e 7 f 8 h 9 b 10 j

Exercise 1

Job Description	Person Specification
main purpose of job reporting relationships location key duties / responsibilities	desirable skills practical requirements previous experience qualifications/training skills and qualities needed for job

Exercise 2
1 Job title
2 Reports to
3 Responsible for
4 Job overview
5 Key duties / responsibilities
6 Essential experience
7 Location

Exercise 3
1 False – the job is based in Manchester and requires a lot of traveling in Great Britain and Northern Ireland
2 False – the training manager is responsible for two administrators, one administrative assistant, and a team of trainers
3 True
4 False – he/she reports directly to the General Manager, UK and Northern Europe
5 True

Exercise 4
1 reports to
2 work, establish
3 evaluate, develop
4 conducting
5 prepare
6 involves

Exercise 5
1 b 2 d 3 f 4 e 5 a 6 c

Exercise 6
1 Qualifications/training
2 Previous experience
3 Skills and qualities needed for job
4 Desirable skills
5 Competencies
6 Additional information

Exercise 7
1 self-starter
2 team-building
3 intercultural awareness
4 quality control
5 decision-maker
6 open lines of communication

Exercise 8
Mentioned: company website, online job portals, in-house recruitment, trade journals
Not mentioned: national/local newspapers, executive search / recruitment agency, job fairs, networking / social media

Exercise 9
1 False – Robert is responsible for this
2 True
3 True
4 True
5 False – candidates must have high-level English skills
6 False – he doesn't think there is much chance of finding someone in-house
7 False – it publishes advertisements, but their circulation is limited and the ads are expensive
8 True
9 False – the merger is not given as the reason for the job search
10 False – she only asks to be kept posted about them

Exercise 10
1 Do you have a moment?
2 They must be highly proficient in English.
3 I'm not sure I agree with you there.
4 I'm one step ahead of you.
5 You clearly have things under control.

Exercise 11
1 g 2 h 3 a 4 e 5 f 6 b 7 d 8 c

A have a word
B has signed off on
C generalist
D internal
E merger
F trade journal
G Keep me posted
H disciplinary procedures

Exercise 12
2 unemployment
3 employer
4 employees
5 employed
6 recruited
7 recruitment
8 recruiting

Exercise 13
1 h 2 g 3 e 4 b 5 f 6 c 7 a 8 d

Exercise 14
Answers will vary.

Unit 2

Warmer
Answers will vary.

Exercise 1
1 e 2 h 3 c 4 g 5 d 6 f 7 b 8 a

Exercise 2
(suggested answers)
1 The main responsibilities are dealing with customer travel needs, promoting JetWing's range of services and general customer service.
2 The hours of work will vary. You'll be working on a shift basis, which includes weekends and bank holidays.
3 Desirable competencies include managing customer demands, teamwork, and attention to detail.
4 Yes, you will receive a shift allowance, which is an additional payment for working outside normal business hours.
5 It will consist of a group interview for 90 minutes, followed by a series of exercises and then an individual interview with two assessors.
6 There's an increase to the base salary after the six-month trial period.

Exercise 3
(suggested answers)
1 Personal Details
2 Personal Profile
3 Professional Experience
4 Skills and Achievements
5 Education
6 Training and Development

Exercise 4
Education: academic qualifications
Skills and Achievements: exceptional performance ratings, language skills, soft skills
Personal Profile: brief summary of work history and abilities
Training and Development: internships, qualifications or certificates from on-the-job training, relevant training courses attended, seminars attended
Professional Experience: dates of previous employment, key achievements in previous positions, previous employers, responsibilities in previous positions
Personal Details: full contact details, nationality

Exercise 5
1 j 2 d 3 g 4 b 5 a 6 i 7 f 8 c 9 h
10 e

Exercise 6
1 False – she applied for a position as call center team leader
2 True
3 False – the initial interview will take place within two weeks
4 True
5 False – details of the assessment center procedure will be sent in advance
6 False – they want her to bring the application form with her to the interview

Exercise 7
1 c 2 a 3 f 4 e 5 d 6 b

Exercise 8
1 phone you to arrange
2 come by, initial
3 Unfortunately
4 though
5 come in
6 let's say
7 fill it in
8 look forward

Exercise 9
Answers will vary.

Exercise 10
1 resigned / handed in her notice / quit
2 hire / take on, notice
3 lay off
4 let go / made redundant / offered early retirement / laid off
5 fired/sacked
6 let go/made redundant/offered early retirement

Exercise 11
five years with present company, eight team leaders, seven days a week, ten call center associates, six years in previous company

Problems discussed: 1, 4

1 A 2 B 3 B 4 A 5 B

Exercise 12
1 b 2 a 3 a 4 b 5 a 6 a

Exercise 13
2 team leader, call center
3 promoted to team leader two years ago
4 six years' experience in customer service
5 responsible for 10 call center associates
6 direct responsibility for difficult customers
7 regular weekly meetings with team leaders, call center staff change teams to gain experience
8 enjoys customer contact
9 part of call center is relocating, doesn't wish to move (children in school / partner working in the same area)
10 seem excellent, she is used to a well-structured call center, and relationships with customers are given top priority.

Exercise 14
(suggested answers)
1 Could you tell me about your relationship with your present supervisor? / How do you get on with …?

2 Could you outline one or two staff problems you have had and how you dealt with them?
3 Could you give some examples of how you have handled customers well?
4 What shift hours do you normally work?
5 Could you give me some examples of decisions you've made on your own initiative?
6 How well do you work under pressure? Could you give some examples?

1 d 2 c 3 e 4 a 5 g 6 b 7 f

Exercise 15
Answers will vary.

Exercise 16
2 application
3 applicable
4 selective
5 selection
6 assessment
7 assess

Unit 3

Warmer
1 sex discrimination (c) 2 employment contract (h)
3 equal pay (e) 4 parental leave (d)
5 workplace injuries (b) 6 short-time working (a)
7 disciplinary and grievance procedure (g)
8 work-related stress (f)

Exercise 1
benefits package – paid vacation – relocation expenses – sick leave – trial/probationary period

Exercise 2
1 False – flexitime is not offered
2 False – overtime work will either be paid or offered in lieu as time off
3 False – after 12 weeks she continues to be paid by an insurance company
4 True
5 True
6 False – her current employer knows she plans to leave

Exercise 3
1 f 2 b 3 a 4 e 5 d 6 c

Exercise 4
1 overtime
2 time off
3 annual
4 contacting
5 subject

Exercise 5
Across: 3 offer, 6 contract, 7 work week, 8 handbook
Down: 1 reference, 2 vacation, 4 present, 5 form

Exercise 6
Work patterns: flextime/flexitime, six-day week
Terms of contract: full-time employment, part-time employment, relocation expense
Time away from work: paid vacation / holiday entitlement, public holiday / bank holiday, sick leave
Ending employment: dismissal, redundancy, resignation

Exercise 7
1 flexible
2 flextime/flexitime
3 flexibility
4 inflexible

Exercise 8
1 e 2 c 3 i 4 g 5 j 6 d 7 a 8 h 9 f 10 b

Exercise 9
2 may be required
3 are expected
4 notified in writing
5 are entitled to
6 payable monthly in arrears
7 are asked
8 subject to disciplinary action

Exercise 10
Offer letter: d – c – i – a – f
Rejection letter: g – b – h – j – e

1 c 2 e 3 h 4 a 5 d 6 f 7 b 8 g

Exercise 11
Answers will vary.

Exercise 12
1 internal, occur
2 statement, conditions
3 accompanied, representative
4 behavior, opportunity

Exercise 13
(suggested answers)
1 More people are taking time off work due to sickness.
2 Women have difficulty getting leadership positions in companies because of the "glass ceiling", an invisible barrier to advancement.
3 There are not enough examples of working fathers with a successful work/life balance.
4 Modern diversity concerns are more complex than skin color.
5 More companies are implementing policies against having or showing tattoos.
6 More and more companies are encouraging staff to look after their health.
7 Some companies believe that younger employees ("millennials") need training in how to behave in the workplace.
8 Companies are increasingly using open-plan offices, though employees don't always like this change.

Exercise 14
Answers will vary.

Exercise 15
Factories: 1, 2, 3, 4, 5, 6, 7, 8
Offices: 1, 3, 4, 7

Unit 4

Warmer
Answers will vary.

Exercise 1
2 secondment
3 individual development
4 performance review
5 equal opportunity policies
6 team development
7 mentoring
8 onboarding process / induction programme

Exercise 2
1 supervisor
2 situation
3 trouble
4 participates
5 colleagues
6 complained
7 regulations
8 courses

1 B 2 D 3 C 4 A

Exercise 3
1 c 2 a 3 e 4 b 5 d

Exercise 4
(suggested answers)
1 Clearly the company has a problem with equal pay. As soon as they clarify the situation, they should ensure that there aren't any other discrepancies like this. They should also check that their equal opportunity policies are in place.
2 They should consider the advantages of introducing some flexible working practices into the company before too many other staff leave. Introducing some sort of flextime system and then looking closely at their parental policies would be good places to start.
3 English training is obviously needed in this company as multinational companies will expect PR people to be proficient in this area. They should consider introducing English training as soon as possible, either on a weekly basis or by offering an intensive workshop.
4 It is essential that the company assesses the suitability and setup of his workstation. Employers are expected to minimize the risk of such illnesses, especially for those who spend a lot of time in front of a computer.

Exercise 5
1 Enhancing performance
2 Succession planning
3 Opening communication channels
4 Engaging staff

Exercise 6
1 False – Marco was on sick leave
2 False – Jordan fell behind due to staffing difficulties
3 False – Anna was away for one month
4 True
5 True
6 True
7 True
8 False – Jordan's wife is happy with her job

Management Skills:
delegate better
have leadership training
time management

Improving Performance:
25% down for six months
get output up to scratch
behind because of staff difficulties

Encouraging Better Communication:
check in with each other more often
meet weekly for a while
raise issues at team meetings

Exercise 7
1 to detail
2 relationships
3 delegate
4 decrease
5 skills
6 long-term sickness
7 overtime
8 communication
9 cultural
10 production director
11 leadership
12 training manager

Exercise 8
1 b 2 f 3 d 4 e 5 a 6 c

Exercise 9
(suggested answers)
2 You were actually 25% down for six months.
3 Why didn't you raise this issue (at the regular team meeting)?
4 I'm concerned you didn't feel able to discuss it with me.
5 The results are not very impressive, Jordan.
6 You need to think about delegating more.
7 I think you and I need to improve our communication.
8 Finally, on a personal note, Jordan, how is your wife settling in?

Exercise 10
Answers will vary.

Exercise 11
1 Leadership and Team Building
2 Time Management
3 Staff Retention Success
4 Team Leading from a Distance

Exercise 12
1 competent
2 inspire
3 targets
4 priorities
5 managing
6 turnover
7 boosting
8 colleagues

Exercise 13
Answers will vary.

Exercise 14
2 inequality
3 Equality
4 diversity
5 diverse

Exercise 15
1 internal change
2 put an end to
3 laying the groundwork
4 once-a-year
5 In its place
6 ongoing basis

Unit 5

Warmer
See Exercise 5 on page 46 for possible answers.

Exercise 1
1 suit/lifestyle
2 pay/tax
3 competitive/package
4 Dual-career/duplicated
5 choosing/benefits
6 sense/control

Exercise 2
1 c 2 a 3 b

Exercise 3
2 h – C 3 d – E 4 g – G 5 f – H 6 c – D
7 a – B 8 e – A

Exercise 4
1 input
2 mean
3 you know
4 fill
5 in favor
6 look

Exercise 5
1 f 2 h 3 k 4 b 5 j 6 c 7 l 8 a 9 d
10 g 11 i 12 e

Exercise 6
2 canteen
3 pension
4 share
5 transferred
6 merit
7 retain
8 classes
Mystery word: benefits

Exercise 7
1 benefit
2 benefits
3 beneficiary
4 reviewed
5 reviews

Exercise 8
Answers will vary.

Exercise 9
1 Best wishes
2 initial
3 recommend
4 information
5 of
6 was
7 offer
8 workforce
Order of sentences: e – c – f – b – d – a

Exercise 10
1 c 2 f 3 d 4 b 5 a 6 e

Corrections to Liam's notes:
there are at least ~~six~~ *two* staff
(those who relocated from ~~Canada~~ *London and New York* last year)
Performance reviews will take place in the ~~new year~~ *November and early December*
Flexitime ~~will be~~ *may be* introduced next year

Upward movement: have a raise, to rise
Downward movement: take a drop, less, be cut

Exercise 11
1 five thousand euros
2 sixty thousand pounds per annum
3 fifty million, two hundred thirty-nine thousand, one hundred (and) fifty dollars
4 seventy billion euros
5 a/one hundred and ten million dollars
6 a/one hundred and fifty pounds per hour

Exercise 12
1 e 2 d 3 a 4 c 5 b 6 f

Unit 6

Warmer
1 True
2 False – the largest union in Germany is IG Metall
3 True
4 True
5 True
6 False – South Africa has one of the highest rates of industrial action due to strikes in the mining sector

Exercise 1
a in a bid
b stagnate
c unlawful
d hike

Exercise 2
1 take industrial action (sentence c)
2 if wages and conditions are not improved (sentence a)
3 forcing the pilots back to work (sentence f)
4 demanding increased pay (sentence e)
5 in a bid for higher wages (sentence d)
6 negotiate a new collective agreement (sentence b)

Exercise 3
1 a 2 c 3 b 4 b 5 c

Exercise 4
1 *behind* – The union wants the same increase as the white-collar workers.
2 *counter* – He said that they had a 3% review a year ago, sales were down and there might have to be redundancies in Amsterdam if things don't improve.
3 *fail, agreement* – The union felt 3% was too low. They want 5%.
4 *freeze* – The company lost a big contract and there was also a recession.
5 *rumors* – The rumors are that work will be transferred to Poland due to an economic downturn in the industry.
6 *tactics* – The last thing they want is a strike and they cannot pay 5%, so a good outcome has to be achieved when they meet the union again.

Exercise 5
1 b 2 a 3 b 4 a 5 b 6 a

Exercise 6
(suggested answers)
1 Prepare your arguments.
2 Be flexible and prepared to compromise.
3 Always remember your aims.
4 Use simple and clear language.
5 Always listen carefully to the other person.
6 Build rapport and be courteous.
7 Be positive – highlight common ground.
8 Be constructive and avoid open conflict.
9 Use persuasion, not threats.
10 When agreement is reached, summarize clearly and close the deal.

Exercise 7
building rapport: 4, 7
establishing objectives and aims: 9, 10
bargaining: 2, 6
addressing conflict: 3, 5
concluding: 1, 8

Exercise 8
1 f – E 2 d – A 3 e – F 4 g – B 5 c – D
6 a – C 7 h – G 8 b – H

1 False – they are expected to get better
2 False – overtime ceased six months ago
3 True
4 True
5 False – management made the statement that there is no plan to close the plant or transfer their jobs to another country
6 True

Exercise 9
1 met
2 are receiving
3 have been / are / were
4 transferring
5 gave
6 was not / wasn't / is not / isn't
7 is not / isn't
8 accepted

Exercise 10
(suggested answers)
2 Provided (that) there is an increase in sales, we can offer a further 2% pay rise.
3 If we don't give a further increase in pay, there will be no job losses in Amsterdam.
4 There will be another review in nine months on condition that there is no industrial action.
5 If productivity increased, we could pay a bonus at the end of the year.
6 Unless we open on Sundays from 10:00 a.m. to 4:00 p.m., we'll lose business to our competitors.
7 Provided (that) customerservice doesn't suffer, we can introduce flexible working hours.

Exercise 11
Answers will vary.

Exercise 12
1 negotiator
2 negotiable
3 negotiation
4 consultant
5 consultation
6 Consulting

Exercise 13
Answers will vary.

Model Correspondence

Invitation to an Interview

To: Heiko Fischer
From: John Spence
Subject: International Marketing Assistant – Manchester

Dear Mr. Fischer,

Thank you for your email of 2 September, applying for the position of International Marketing Assistant with this company.

We would like to invite you to attend an interview at this office. I would be grateful if you could call me at 0044 0675 23144 as soon as possible to arrange a suitable time.

Attached is a copy of the person specification and job description, which we would like you to familiarize yourself with before the interview. Alternatively, you can go to our website for these documents and other information about the company. A map showing the location of our office is also attached.

If you have any questions, please raise them when you call to arrange the interview. We look forward to meeting you.

Yours sincerely,
John Spence

Notice of Rejection

To: George McAllister
From: John Spence
Subject: International Marketing Assistant – Manchester

Dear Mr. McAllister,

Thank you for your email of 4 September, applying for the position of International Marketing Assistant.

We have reviewed your application but regret that we are unable to offer you an interview at this time.

We wish you every success and appreciate your interest in our company.

Yours sincerely,
John Spence

Notice of Rejection (after the first interview)

To: Alexandra Bang
From: William Cartridge
Subject: International Marketing Assistant – Manchester

Dear Ms. Bang,

Thank you for attending the interview on 17 September for the position of International Marketing Assistant. It was very nice meeting you.

We have now fully considered your application and regret that we are unable to offer you the position on this occasion. At your request, we can hold your details pending and let you know if a suitable opening occurs in the future.

We appreciate your interest in our company and would like to take this opportunity of wishing you every success.

Yours sincerely,
William Cartridge

26 Lymington Road
Manchester M34 2RD
Tel: 0044 0675 23144
Fax: 0044 0675 23145
businesssystems-ltd.co.uk

Business Systems Ltd

20 September 20...

Mr. Heiko Fischer
Mouse Cottage
Green Lane
Sevenoaks
Kent TN15 2AP

Dear Mr. Fischer,

International Marketing Assistant – Manchester

Further to your recent interviews, we are pleased to offer you the position of International Marketing Assistant in the UK Marketing Department, based at this address, at a commencing salary of £42,000 per annum. This offer is conditional on receiving a satisfactory reference from your present and last employers and to the satisfactory completion of a three-month probationary period.

Basic hours of work are 9:00 a.m. to 6:00 p.m., Monday to Friday, including an hour for lunch. It will be necessary for you to work overtime as and when required. Holiday entitlement is 20 days per annum, rising to 25 after two years' service. Normally holiday cannot be taken during the probationary period. All terms, conditions, and benefits are detailed in the handbook and contract enclosed.

We would like you to start on 1 November, if possible. During your first week you will participate in an induction seminar to familiarize you fully with the company. Full details of this will be sent to you nearer the time.

Please let us know as soon as possible if you would like to accept by signing and returning one copy of the contract. We will then take up references. We hope you will join us and very much look forward to hearing from you.

Yours sincerely,

June Stewart

June Stewart
Head of International HR

encs
Contract of employment
Company handbook

Request for a Reference

26 Lymington Road
Manchester M34 2RD
Tel: 0044 0675 23144
Fax: 0044 0675 23145
businesssystems-ltd.co.uk

Business Systems Ltd

25 September 20...

Glenda Martin
Human Resources Manager
Greenman International Books
25 Manning Avenue
Glasgow G23 6RT

Dear Ms. Martin,

Re: Heiko Fischer

The above-named is being considered for the post of International Marketing Assistant and has indicated that you would be willing to provide a reference. I would therefore be grateful if you would confirm to me his position and the dates he was employed by your company.

Any information you can give as to Mr. Fischer's suitability for the above type of position would be helpful, and will be treated in the strictest confidence. I am enclosing a job description and person specification for the position he is being considered for.

We would appreciate your prompt reply.

Yours sincerely,

June Stewart

June Stewart
Head of International HR

encs

Reference

Greenman International Books
25 Manning Avenue
Glasgow G23 6RT
Tel: 0044 0141 628749
Fax: 0044 0141 628750
www.greenmanint.co.uk

June Stewart
Head of International HR
Business Systems Ltd
26 Lymington Road
Manchester M34 2RD

28 September 20..

Dear Ms. Stewart,

Re: Heiko Fischer

I'm writing in response to your letter of 25 September asking for a reference on behalf of the above. Heiko Fischer was employed by this company from 1 January 2008 until 31 October 2014, when he left of his own accord. We understand he was proposing to travel for four months in Australia. He started as a trainee in our Public Relations department and transferred to Marketing in April 2010 where he worked as a Marketing Assistant. During his time in our employ he consistently met expectations and worked to our satisfaction in all areas. His involvement in international affairs covered the last two years of his employment.

We are delighted to give a reference for Mr. Fischer and have no reason to believe he would not be suitable for the job outlined in your enclosures. We wish him well in his future career.

This reference is given without responsibility on the part of the writer and the company.

Yours sincerely,

Glenda Martin

Glenda Martin
Human Resources Manager

Phrases to Use

The phrases below will be useful tools in your work. Highlight phrases that are particularly relevant to you and look at them regularly to help you remember them.

Job interviews

Establishing rapport and relaxing the candidate

Thanks for taking the time to come in today.
Perhaps we can start with you walking me through your resume.
Please feel free to ask any questions you may have.
I'm going to start by … and then we'll talk about …
Finally, we can deal with any points you would like to raise.

Giving information

I'd like to tell you something about …
Please ask about anything you are not sure of.
I'm sure that won't be a problem …
I'm afraid we don't …

Questions

What experience have you had with …?
What aspect of your job do you like best?
How would you handle …?
How do you go about dealing with …?
Why do you want to leave your present job?

Asking Follow-up Questions

Could you tell me a little more about …?
What exactly do you mean by … ?
Could you expand on that?

Performance reviews

Review questions

What do you like most about your work?
Could you tell me (how things are going with …)?
How do you see (your team developing in …)?
Would you like to give me more details about …?
When did you realize that …?
Would you mind giving me more information on …?
Is there anything else we should talk about?

Talking about problems

I'd like you to tell me how you see your progress over the last year.
Has there been anything you have found difficult to cope with?
How are things with the rest of the department?

Softening disagreement

With (all due) respect, I think …
To be quite frank, I don't think …
In all honesty, we should deal with that differently …
I respect your opinion, but …
I'm afraid we can't / I'm sorry but we can't …
You have a point there, but …
To a certain extent I agree, but …

Negotiating

Persuading

It would be to your advantage to ...
It might be in your interest to …
We can reassure you on that point totally.
It's the best offer around. You won't find a better one.

Bargaining

We would agree on one condition.
If you agree to …, we can …
If you threaten to strike, we'll withdraw the offer.
If you stopped picketing, then I think we could make a counteroffer.
We might put a better offer on the table, provided (that) you stop the strike.
I'd go along with that on the condition that you returned to work.
That seems to be a good compromise, as long as there is no industrial action of any kind.
Unless your members return to work tomorrow, we'll withdraw our offer.

Arranging an appointment

What date would be convenient for you?
What time would suit you / works for you?
Would Monday at 10:30 suit you / work?
Is March 5th at 6:00 p.m. convenient?
How about 10:00 a.m.?
Tuesday the 8th of July would be good for me.
Monday's bad for me, I'm afraid.
That sounds great.
Yes, that would be good for me.
I think that should be possible.

Exchanging information

Can we have a word about …?
I'd like to be up to date on what's happening.
So where/what are you planning to …?
What are you your thoughts on …?

Asking for someone's opinion

What's your view on this?
Could I have your input, Alex?

Giving an opinion or feedback

Yes, I think we need …
Well, I'm definitely in favor of …
Good idea.
However, I think we should also look closely at …

Agreeing and disagreeing

I agree. / I disagree.
I entirely agree.
Thanks, that's a great point.
I agree with you to a point.
Yes, but have you considered …?
I'm afraid I can't go along with that.
I'm not sure I agree with you there.
Sorry, but I really can't agree.

Making recommendations and suggestions

We need to introduce …
My proposal is to put / is that we put …
Maybe we should also look into …
I propose introducing / that we introduce …
It's essential to take up / that we take up references …
We still need to …
I (can) recommend talking / that we talk …
It's high time (that) we introduced …
I suggest we …
In my opinion …
What do you think about …?
Well, we should consider …

Clarifying

What exactly do you mean by …?
As you know, we need …
I'll fill you in on …

Interrupting

Could I just say that ...?
I'd like to add a point here.
Excuse me, can I just come in here?
Sorry, but may I just clarify a point before we go on?

Key Verbs in Context

to assess	Without interviewing someone, it can be difficult to assess if they will be right for the job.	beurteilen, einschätzen
to clarify	Questions about the job can be clarified at the interview.	klären
to conduct	My interview was conducted by the head of HR.	führen
to consider	What would you consider to be your greatest strength?	betrachten
to contribute	What do you feel you could contribute to our company?	beitragen
to cope	Without sufficient support, it can be difficult to cope with challenging situations.	zurechtkommen
to dismiss	Dismissing people is never easy, but that's part of the job.	entlassen
to employ	Our company employs over 2,000 individuals worldwide.	beschäftigen
to enable	An assistant would enable me to focus on my main tasks.	ermöglichen
to encourage	I encourage you to come and speak to us if you have any problems.	unterstützen
to fire	We had to fire her as she was not doing her job properly.	hinauswerfen, feuern
to hand in one's notice/resignation	He's threatening to hand in his notice if the situation doesn't improve.	kündigen
to handle	How would you handle the problem?	umgehen mit
to hire	We need to hire a new administrative assistant as our current one has handed in his notice.	einstellen
to implement	We've implemented a new training course, and it's a great improvement over the old one.	einführen
to let go	The recent merger means that, unfortunately, we'll have to let some people go.	gehen lassen
to maintain	We monitor the progress of new employees very closely.	kontrollieren
to monitor	We monitor the progress of new employees very closely.	kontrollieren
to notify	You will be notified in writing of any changes to your contract.	benachrichtigen
to persuade	I persuaded him to stay by promising that we would find a solution to the communication problems.	überreden
to recruit	We like to recruit enthusiastic, creative people.	einstellen
to reject	Badly written and unorganized CVs are rejected immediately.	ablehnen
to report to s.o.	You will report directly to the head of the IT department.	jdm. unterstellt sein
to resign	Three members of the team have resigned in the last two years.	kündigen
to resolve	My favorite aspect of the job is resolving problems and helping colleagues work together better.	lösen
to retain	If we're having trouble retaining staff, we need to look at our HR policies.	halten
to settle in	It always takes some time to settle in to a new job.	(sich) einarbeiten
to take effect	Changes to employment law will take effect next month.	in Kraft treten
to take s.o. on	They took me on because I had a lot of relevant experience.	jdm. einstellen
to value	We value our employees and show this through the salary and benefits we offer.	schätzen

A–Z Wordlist

A

ability Fähigkeit, Können
absenteeism Abwesenheit
access Zugang
to **accompany** begleiten
according to laut, nach
accuracy Genauigkeit
to **achieve** erreichen, erzielen
acknowledgement Bestätigung
to **adjust** anpassen
to **afford** sich leisten (können)
to **agree** festlegen, vereinbaren
to **amend** (ab)ändern
annual jährlich
anxiety Angst(zustand)
applicable zutreffend
applicant Bewerber/in
application Bewerbung
appraisal Bewertung
to **appreciate sth.** etw. zu schätzen wissen
aptitude Befähigung
argumentative streitsüchtig
to **assess** beurteilen
assessment Bewertung
assurances Zusicherung, Zusagen
audit Prüfung
awareness Bewusstsein

B

bank holiday (BE) öffentlicher Feiertag
bankruptcy Bankrott, Konkurs
to **bargain** verhandeln
base salary Grundgehalt
beneficiary Begünstigte/r
benefits Sozialleistungen
blue-collar worker Arbeiter
board (of directors) Vorstand
bonus Zulage, Prämie, Bonus
bottom line Endergebnis
branch Filiale
bullying Mobbing

C

to **carry out** durchführen
childcare Kinderbetreuung
to **clarify** (näher) erläutern, klären
closed shop gewerkschaftspflichtiger Betrieb
closure Schließung
collective agreement Tarifvereinbarung, Manteltarif
commencing salary Anfangsgehalt
compensation Entschädigung, Abfindung
competency Kompetenz, Fähigkeit
competent kompetent, fähig
competitor Konkurrent/in, Konkurrenz
to **complain** sich beklagen
complaint Beanstandung, Reklamation
complimentary close Schlussformel
concessionary ermäßigt
to **conduct** durchführen
conscious bewusst
considerably wesentlich
to **consist of** bestehen aus
consistent einheitlich, gleichbleibend
to **consult** (sich) beraten
consultant Berater/in
consultation Beratung
to **contain** unter Kontrolle bringen
contract Vertrag
to **contribute** beitragen
convenient passend, günstig
to **convince** überzeugen
to **cope with sth.** mit etw. klarkommen
counseling Beratung
counter-argument Gegenargument
counteroffer Gegenangebot
curriculum vitae / CV (BE) Lebenslauf

D

daycare Kinderbetreuung
to **deal with sth.** sich um etw. kümmern
decrease Rückgang
defined-benefit scheme leistungsorientiertes System
defined-contribution scheme Beitragsprimat
degree (akademischer) Abschluss
to **deliver** liefern
dependable zuverlässig
dependent Angehörige/r
to **detail** detailliert aufführen
to **determine** bestimmen
dignity Würde
directive Anordnung, Direktive
disability Behinderung
disciplinary action/procedure Disziplinarverfahren
to **discriminate against** diskriminieren
to **dismiss** entlassen

dismissal Entlassung, Freisetzung
to **disregard** vernachlässigen
to **downsize** (sich) verkleinern, Stellen abbauen
to **drag one's feet** hinterherhinken
due to wegen, aufgrund von
duties Aufgaben, Pflichten

E

to **employ** an-/einstellen, beschäftigen
employee Arbeitnehmer/in, Angestellte/r
employer Arbeitgeber/in
to **empower** stärken
to **enable** ermöglichen
to **enclose** beilegen, beifügen
to **encourage** fördern, unterstützen
to **endorse** befürworten
to **engage** einstellen
to **ensure** gewährleisten
equal opportunity policy Chancengleichheit
equally gleichmäßig
to **establish** aufbauen
to **evaluate** beurteilen
to **expand (on sth.)** mehr ins Detail gehen
experience (Berufs-)Erfahrung

F

failure to do sth. bei Nichteinhaltung
faithful treu
to **familiarize** vertraut machen
fast-paced schnelllebig
field (of work) Arbeitsbereich
to **finalize** endgültig festlegen
to **fire (AE)** feuern, hinauswerfen
first aid erste Hilfe
flexitime (BE) Gleitzeit
flextime (AE) Gleitzeit
folder Mappe
form Formular
formality Förmlichkeit
to **foster** fördern, unterstützen
fringe benefits zusätzliche Sozialleistungen

G

gender Geschlecht
grievance Beschwerde

H

to **hand in one's resignation/notice** kündigen
harassment Belästigung
to **have a word** kurz sprechen
hearing Anhörung
high time höchste Zeit
hike Steigerung
to **hire** ein-/anstellen
to **hold s.o. accountable** jmd zur Verantwortung ziehen
holiday Feiern, Urlaub
holiday entitlement (BE) Urlaubsanspruch
hot under the collar wütend

I

to **implement** umsetzen, einführen
in a bid in dem Versuch
in arrears rückwirkend
incentive Anreiz
in-depth detailliert
induction programme (BE) Einführungsprogramm
industrial action Arbeitskampf(maßnahmen), Ausstand
in-house innerbetrieblich
insurance Versicherung
internship Praktikum
interpersonal relationships zwischenmenschliche Beziehung
interpersonal skills der Umgang mit anderen Leuten
interview Ein-/Vorstellungsgespräch
intimidation Einschüchterung
to **involve** umfassen

J

job description Stellenbeschreibung
job fair Jobbörse, Berufsmesse

K

to **keep s.o. posted** auf dem Laufenden halten
knowledgeable kenntnisreich

L

labor union (AE) Gewerkschaft
to **lay off** (zeitweilig) entlassen
to **let s.o. go** jmd. gehen lassen
to **liaise** in Kontakt sein
to **look forward to** sich freuen auf
to **look into sth.** etw. prüfen

M

to **maintain** aufrechterhalten
to **make redundant** entlassen
to **manage** leiten
manual Handbuch
maternity leave Mutterschutz, Elternzeit (für die Mutter)
mentoring Mentorenbetreuung
merger Fusion
merit basis auf Leistung basiert
mileage allowance Kilometergeld

monetary terms finanzielle Hinsicht
to **monitor** kontrollieren
to **muddle through** sich durchwursteln

N

to **negotiate** ver-/aushandeln
negotiation Verhandlung
negotiator Verhandlungsführer
non-contributory beitragsfrei
non-negotiable unumstößlich
to **notify** benachrichtigen

O

to **occur** vorkommen
offer letter Angebotsschreiben
onboarding process (AE) Einführungsprogramm
on the contrary im Gegenteil
on the horizon in Sicht
outlook Aussichten, Ausblick
to **outsource** auslagern, outsourcen
overdue überfällig
to **oversee** beaufsichtigen, leiten
overtime Überstunden

P

paid vacation (AE) Urlaubsanspruch
parental leave Elternzeit
payable zahlbar, fällig
pension Rente, Pension
pensioner Rentner
people skills soziale Kompetenz
per annum pro Jahr
performance review Mitarbeitergespräch, Leistungsbeurteilung
performance-based erfolgsabhängig
perk betriebliche/freiwillige Sozialleistung
person specification Anforderungsprofil
to **persuade** überzeugen
to **picket** Streikposten stehen
to **play sth. down** etw. herunterspielen
predecessor Vorgänger
preferable vorzuziehen
probationary period Probezeit
proficient kompetent
profit-sharing Gewinnbeteiligung
promotion Beförderung
to **provide** zur Verfügung stellen
to **pursue** verfolgen, nachgehen
to **put into effect** verwirklichen
to **put one's cards on the table** Farbe bekennen

Q

to **quit** kündigen

R

raise (AE) (Gehalts-)Erhöhung
range Sortiment, Angebot
rapport (enges) Verhältnis
to **react to** reagieren auf
to **reassure** versichern, beruhigen
to **recruit** rekrutieren, einstellen
recruitment Einstellung (von Arbeitskräften)
recurring wiederkehrend
redundancy Entlassung, Freisetzung
referee Referenzgeber/in
reference Referenz, (Arbeits-)Zeugnis
to **refuse to** sich weigern
to **reject** ablehnen
rejection (letter) Absage
relationship Beziehung, Verhältnis
reliable zuverlässig
to **relocate** an einen anderen (Stand-)Ort ziehen
relocation expense Umzugskosten
remuneration Vergütung, Bezahlung
renowned renommiert
to **report to s.o.** jmd. Rapport erstatten
reporting relationship Stellung im Unternehmen
to **require** erfordern, erforderlich machen
to **resign** kündigen
resignation Kündigung(sschreiben)
to **resolve** lösen
resourcefulness Einfallsreichtum
resourceful einfallsreich
responsible verantwortlich
resume (AE) Lebenslauf
to **retain** beibehalten, erhalten
to **retire** in den Ruhestand treten
retirement Ruhestand
to **reveal** aufzeigen
to **revise** revidieren, überarbeiten
reward entlohnen
rise (BE) (Gehalts-)Erhöhung

S

to **sack** feuern, hinauswerfen
salary Gehalt, Lohn
satisfactory zufriedenstellend, befriedigend
secondment Einsatz an einem anderen (Stand-)Ort
to **select** auswählen
self-employed selbstständig
sensitivity Sensibilität
to **settle in** sich einleben
severe schwer
sex discrimination Geschlechterdiskriminierung
share (Geschäfts-)Anteil, Aktie
shift allowance Schichtzuschlag
shift pattern Schichtplan

shop floor Produktionsstätte, Werkstatt
shop steward Betriebsratsvorsitzender
short-time work Kurzarbeit
shortage Mangel
to **shortlist** in die engere Auswahl ziehen
sick leave Genesungsurlaub
to **sign off on sth.** etw. genehmigen
to **slash** (drastisch) reduzieren
stage Etappe
statement of intent Absichtserklärung
to **streamline** rationalisieren
strike streiken
to **submit** einreichen, vorstellen
to **subsidize** subventionieren
succession planning Nachfolgeplanung
successor Nachfolger
suggestion Vorschlag
suitable geeignet, passend, angemessen
supervisor Abteilungsleiter/in
to **support** unterstützen
survey Umfrage
to **swap** (aus)tauschen

T

tailor-made maßgeschneidert
to **take effect** in Kraft treten
to **take into account** berücksichtigen
to **take on** übernehmen, einstellen
to **take sides** Partei ergreifen
target Ziel(vorgaben)
tedious lästig, ermüdend
to **terminate** (Vertrag) auflösen/beenden
threat Drohung
to **threaten** drohen
trade journal Handelsblatt
trade union (BE) Gewerkschaft
trial period Probezeit
to **turn down** ablehnen

U

to **undertake** unternehmen
union Gewerkschaft
union representative Gewerkschaftsvertreter/in
unlawful rechtswidrig
unsolicited application Blindbewerbung
up to date auf dem Laufenden
up to scratch den Anforderungen entsprechen

V

vacation (AE) Urlaub
to **value** schätzen
value Wert
vast riesengroß
victimization Schikanierung
vulnerable gefährdet

W

white-collar worker (Büro-)Angestellte
to **withdraw (an offer)** (ein Angebot) zurückziehen
work council Betriebsrat
workforce Belegschaft
workload Arbeitsbelastung
works council Betriebsrat

Y

yardstick Maßstab

Tracklist

Track	Unit	Exercise	Running time
01	Title/Copyright		0:51
02	Unit 1	Exercise 8	2:38
03	Unit 2	Exercise 8	1:57
04	Unit 2	Exercise 11 – Part 1	1:03
05	Unit 2	Exercise 11 – Part 2	1:20
06	Unit 2	Exercise 11 – Part 3	0:49
07	Unit 3	Exercise 2	3:54
08	Unit 3	Exercise 12	2:02
09	Unit 4	Exercise 2 – 1	0:29
10	Unit 4	Exercise 2 – 2	0:20
11	Unit 4	Exercise 2 – 3	0:25
12	Unit 4	Exercise 2 – 4	0:16
13	Unit 4	Exercise 6	3:51
14	Unit 5	Exercise 2	1:59
15	Unit 5	Exercise 10	2:12
16	Unit 6	Exercise 3	2:04
17	Unit 6	Exercise 8	4:22
Total running time			30:32

Aufnahmestudio: Andovar Pte. Ltd.